IMMORTAL
MARTYR

Wesley Bartlett

ISBN 978-1-63814-695-7 (Paperback)
ISBN 978-1-63814-696-4 (Digital)

Covenant Books, Inc.
11661 Hwy 707
Murrells Inlet, SC 29576
www.covenantbooks.com

CONTENTS

There I stood on the balcony three stories up overlooking Madison Ave and about to end my life and end the pain once and for all, but then…

Rewind<<<

CHAPTER 1

FALLEN

I grew up in church and was a goody-goody kid for most of my childhood. I was creative, and I loved art and reading. I have severe attention deficit hyperactivity disorder. ADHD is basically like not just having random thoughts that acted as distractions but getting excited about every random thought that acted as distractions. School was only easy if I could focus, which rarely happened; so I was prescribed various different drugs to help, but they had bad side effects. I would lie awake at night for hours with my mind racing, and this made school very difficult because I wasn't getting adequate sleep. I always procrastinated to do the things I needed to do—schoolwork, chores, etc. I grew up in East Memphis, and I had a couple of friends while I lived there. I relentlessly played video games all day, every day. I need to do everything to the extreme because that's just who I am. I would beat video games 100 percent. Every single coin/gem/ achievement and every hidden Easter egg must be found. I loved to create things and build, and I also loved to collect things like rocks, knives, energy drink cans, SoBe bottles, and coins. I loved collecting these things while out on long road trips with my dad while he was working in logistics/deliveries.

At the age of twelve, I was sexually molested by a childhood friend (whom I've now forgiven and asked God to bless) and introduced to pornography around the same time. I didn't know what was demonic or not at that age, but Satan filled my mind from that point on. I was never forced to do anything sexual, but I was seduced to exchange sexual favors. It wasn't even a male attraction, just the desire for pleasure. I was feeding a lust that would eventually consume my life, and I didn't know it yet. Pornography and masturbation became an addiction for eight years. What was worse than that was my deceptive ways. I buried my wicked actions in deceit, thinking, "I'll just hide my addiction and all my wrongdoings so that I'll never have to lie." I was so careful about the timing, and I wasn't stupid about it. I'm so ashamed of that now.

Pornography actually affects the brain like drugs, cigarettes, and gambling. It floods the brain with what experts call the "feel good" chemical—dopamine. Dopamine is naturally produced by the brain when a person sees a friend they like to spend time with, see a movie they like, go to a place they like, or when they eat their favorite food. Pornography overloads the receptors in the brain with so much dopamine that people literally get "high" on its effects. Over time, this actually damages and warps the receptors of the brain, changing the pathways that the neurons are supposed to naturally fire with, and when the pathways fire differently, it can result in permanent brain damage. A brain with warped pathways no longer produces dopamine when normal and natural events are supposed to cause it to. The dopamine high gets weaker after the first few times of watching pornography, and in order to achieve the same high, a person must watch more taboo porn. This progresses into a very difficult addiction to break free from. I was so opened up to demons through immorality, pornography, music, horror movies, lying, deceit, dark humor, and corrupting others. I enjoyed perverting other people's minds with sexual immorality. I had many desires back then that I recognize now to not be my own desires at all but the desires of the demons living in me and influencing me.

Pornography and masturbation were the first major sins, and these led to R-rated movies with other sinful activities in them. Violence, drug use, horror, perversion, and sexual immorality in movies opened the door to violent, horrible, and perverted thoughts all the time and crippling fear. It ruled my mind. Demons wouldn't allow my mind to be innocent or feel normal happiness.

Middle school is when I started listening to secular metal and extreme metal, which let in more demons through my ear gates and created more violent and morbid thoughts. Wicked and perverse lyrics flowed into my subconscious mind and my spirit. I started with opening up to bands like Lamb of God ironically. Then I started expanding into other subgenres of metal. I loved Korn, Slipknot, Disturbed, and Nu Metal starting out. I eventually got into the heavier genres of secular bands like death metal, black metal, deathcore, grindcore, and other extreme metal subgenres. I stumbled upon and was introduced to underground bands that had their own unique sound that no other band could replicate, and I became addicted to seeking out and downloading underground music. If there was something talented out there, I *needed* to hear it. I downloaded thousands of albums and had a few hundred gigabytes of metal on my first computer. I got into death and black metal from Sweden, Finland, Norway, Australia, Poland, Belgium, Germany, and many more and had a massive collection. I had no idea how many demons I had invited in through these mostly evil and Satanic bands. The desktop computer crashed though, and I lost most of it. I still had physical CDs though, and on a church trip, I decided to ride in the church bus with friends. My parents were looking through the CD case that I had left in their car; and I had Disturbed, Eminem, Korn, Slipknot, and many others with vulgar lyrics. So my parents got rid of them, which was God protecting me. I was persistent though. I bought an iPod from a friend and re-downloaded all the same music that got stolen and so much more.

I was an introvert for my teens. I loved going to church and interacting with people even though I was deeply hurting inside and felt so worthless and condemned. I had no hope and had a void in my soul that I would soon try much harder to fill. I had friends that would come over and they would smoke weed, but I never had the desire to join them. I stayed to myself and consumed my time with my addictions. I loved doing wild and crazy things even though completely sober.

At my fifteenth birthday, things got a little out of hand, so to speak. I was walking home from school with a few friends from school, and this dog from the neighborhood followed us and we didn't think anything of it. My party had begun, and a lot of friends and their friends were there and we became bored. So we decided to blow up a spray paint can. First thing that comes to mind, right? We got an old weight plate and set it in the yard with the can on it, and we removed the top spray piece and put some gasoline on it and trailed a fifteen- to twenty-foot line of gasoline to light on fire to be safe, you know? We got out a camera to record it and lit the trail. It burned to the can really quick and we were all at a safe distance from the can, and when it burned down into the can, the fire that shot out was twenty to thirty feet high! It sounded exactly like a jet car from the race shows, and the flames were so hot that it was blowing the tree limbs to sway from the wind of the heat. That was really cool but we weren't done yet. We walked out into the cove and my friend had a can of Axe body spray, so he drew a penis on the ground and lit it on fire. We all walked down the cove and were just having a good time, and the old people in the neighborhood were pretty scared from the fire and from the large amount of people walking down the cove in the middle of the night, so they called the police. We saw blue lights coming, and everyone started taking off back up the cove to the house as quickly as possible. Two of my friends got left behind because they didn't run right away. They were ducking and dodging the police cars that were coming to investigate. They hid behind trees and rolled around on the ground behind bushes to not be seen by police, and both were never caught. The police came up to the house and shined a spotlight on the upstairs window to my game room. My friend opened the window and stuck his head out so they know now we are there and everyone was upstairs in the dark laying on the floor like we weren't there. I or someone else went out to talk to the police. They just said we scared the neighbors and that we were out past curfew so we told them we would stay inside and we were off the hook.

At some point in the night during all this, the dog that followed us home had gotten into my guinea pig cage that was outside under the carport and was playing with my guinea pig Spooky like a play toy, and I found my guinea pig in the yard and he was too hurt to survive. I was really sad. The rest of the night we didn't do anything too crazy. Some of my friends were smoking weed, but I still was sober at that time. Needless to say, a few of my friends were never allowed to my house again after that night.

CHAPTER 2

PHARMAKEIA

I was around drugs a good bit but still hadn't touched them until one day when I decided to try huffing Air Duster for fun. It would drop the tone of voice down a few decibels and give you a strong high. It's extremely dangerous to inhale CO_2 because it can possibly freeze the inside of your lungs, but for us, it was just "fun." We went to Walmart and were acting like fools. My friend peed on the rugs in one of the aisles, and my other friend inhaled some Air Duster and yelled out with a deep monotone voice "Dying fetus!" He was running down the aisle and blacked out and hit the floor, and we got that on film. Air Duster was a wild experience, but it was only the beginning.

I was open to so many demons that at the age of eighteen, I started drinking, smoking weed, and smoking cigarettes at the same time. Just to try it since I became the "legal" age to destroy myself. I was only smoking cigarettes and weed at first. The buzz I got from cigarettes felt so good to numb my pain. I would hold in the cigarette smoke to get a stronger buzz because if I wanted to feel something, I would endure whatever was necessary to achieve it. I started smoking casually with friends from high school, and this was still the early stages of the party lifestyle.

I became good friends with drug dealers, and I would bring them customers and they would smoke me out with weed in return.

What started as a social thing to get together with friends became much more than that. The more I smoked, the less I cared because I was able to numb the deep severe pain I felt daily.

I started drinking shortly after I started smoking cigarettes and weed. The first time was amazing, and I had never felt anything like it before. It was so sublime and this set off an addiction that would destroy my life. I became a hardcore party animal. My whole life I've done everything to the extreme, so partying was no different. I was living a double life until the dark one took control completely. I was an alcoholic, pothead, and drug addict. What started casually for some harmless "fun" eventually lead to chasing after feelings that had me hooked. My motivation for everything was partying, drugs, and alcohol.

I would drink fast, very fast. I chased unattainable happiness and satisfaction through alcohol. I just wanted to keep numbing the pain and I didn't even know the source of that pain yet. I couldn't just drink casually. It was all about the feeling of being drunk. I loved drinking with my best friends and jamming out and doing freestyle metal vocals. It was something I could pour my passion into.

I started playing the PC game League of Legends with some friends, and smoking weed, drinking alcohol, and playing League of Legends were my three favorite things to do for a long time, especially with my friends all in the same room. Games and music were very addicting, but my true motivation was pain and shame. I kept drinking and drinking and drinking. Beer, liquor, wine, mixed drinks, martinis, Jell-O shots, Everclear, moonshine, etc., I didn't care what it was. It was only a medium to achieve the numbness I was chasing after. I went to countless parties and made a fool of myself. I would also drink so fast that I would skip buzzing and tipsy and would go straight to black out drunk every time. I broke the law so many times during this haze of a lifestyle. I would put on the pure churchgoing mask and say all the right things, but I was always chasing my addictions, no matter what the cost. I started building a major tolerance to alcohol and would knock back multiple shots and then go to the store and buy a twelve-pack of beer to keep drinking. I would wake up the next morning with a stomach full of alcohol still just as drunk as the night before. Complete debauchery. I was always a loving person even though I was hurting and this is why I had so many friends. I would never do my friends wrong and I had no desire to hurt them, only myself. I would slam forty ounce beers like it was nothing and only have a buzz, just getting started. I would do keg stands and show off all the time for girls. Thankfully I blacked out so many times that I didn't get the chance to hook up with those girls. God would protect me though too.

I and two friends were on our way to his college, and we had weed and paraphernalia in the car with us. We were in Fayette County, Tennessee, on a back road to avoid the main highway. I was stoned and wasn't speeding, but the speed limit dropped from forty-five to thirty for a short time, and sure enough, there was a cop waiting. When we were pulled over, he asked if we had anything and God intervened and made us all say "No." The cop then asked if he could search the car, and we all said "Yes." I had so much junk in that car, haha. My trunk was full of clothes, knives, swords, and throwing stars from my weapon collection, and the cops were just throwing them out on the ground. They searched all of us, and I had some blunt roaches in my cigarette pack and my other friend had weed on him too. So they cuffed me and him and our other friend dropped his weed on the ground and kicked it under the car. He was slick and didn't get caught. They immediately found in the center console of the car, the ceramic pig salt shaker that I had carved into a pipe to smoke with and we were caught red handed. My friend who didn't get caught waited on us to leave and picked his weed up from under the car after they had searched him and put it back in his pocket. The officer even gave him a ride back to Germantown with a dog in the back barking the whole time and the officer yelling "Shut up!" I have no idea what would have happened had we made it to that college, but I know that God protected me from whatever it was. I arrived at jail and pushed my septum piercing up in my nose so no one could see it and broke a toothpick to put through my eyebrow and lip piercings. It was one large room, and it wasn't a bad experience because I was with my good friend. I then had to make the phone call to my parents. They knew I was smoking weed because they caught me one night with a *whole* pan of banana pudding on the table in my room and me asleep on the couch. They didn't understand my motivations at that time or how bad I truly was. They told me they would let me smoke, but if I ever got arrested, they wouldn't bail me out. But due to their love and mercy, they bailed me out the next day. I had to get a lawyer next, and later down the road after the case was said and done, everything was dismissed entirely because of God's riches of grace.

I still didn't stop drinking though. That only became worse. I would drink until I puked and then drink more. I would intentionally drink on an empty stomach to feel it faster. I would knock back vodka straight from the bottle and could hold my own until I blacked out. I fell into fornication around this time, and I deeply regret hurting those girls by fulfilling my lusts.

I eventually progressed to pills, cough syrup, skeletal muscle relaxers, salvia, Xanax, Lortabs, Percocets, codeine syrup, and spice (synthetic marijuana). I even tried ecstasy, cocaine, shrooms, and bath salts. I only did cocaine, ecstasy, and shrooms a few times; but the worst was bath salts. I'm so thankful I did a tiny amount of it because it was a horrible experience, complete paranoia, and impending doom. It felt like the world was ending, and I could do nothing to stop it. However, Xanax ruined my mind. I abused it bad snorting huge lines and mounds of it and blacking out after mixing it with alcohol.

Abusing it that way gave me suicidal thoughts, anxious feelings, lack of sleep, and made me schizophrenic. I was hearing voices in my head clearly describing how I should kill myself and others all the time. Then, on top of that drug damage, the underground secular metal got darker and more evil, which continued inviting demons in until I was really sick in the head. My porn addiction was getting into much worse types, and at the same time, I searched for the most controversial movies ever made and I tried to download whatever sounded like it would shock me the most because my heart was really wicked and perverted by this point.

I would read lyrics of music that was completely depraved and demonic. Perversion and violence filled my mind, so it was back to that bottle again because it was my best friend.

High school was such a blur, so many drugs, parties, and so much sin. I would destroy myself with alcohol but just kept going back to it. I couldn't stop drinking.

One night on New Year's eve at a party, we decided to make some "tank." For those of you who don't know, tank is a mixed drink of one handle of vodka, one pint of Everclear, twenty-four beers, and lemonade and limeade concentrate. It tasted like fruit juice but destroyed people. The reason it is called tank is because you have to be a tank to handle drinking it. The night was young, and since I was helping to host the party, we got to drink the tank first. I had five glasses of it, and I mixed it with some McChicken sandwiches to absorb the alcohol. This worked for a few hours, but as the night progressed, I kept drinking, and the last thing I remember was drinking my Budweiser in a kitchen full of people, and right when the ball dropped for the new year, I blacked out. There was a problem though. We each snorted a huge five- to six-inch line of Adderall before the night began because that would keep me awake to drink whatever I wanted, right? Definitely not. I still blacked out drunk, just not my mind. My mind was out but I was still very much conscious.

I woke up later that night around 4:00 a.m. with a busted lip, bruises *all* over my body, and layer upon layer of green, yellow, and blue Sharpie on my face and body. I was naked, wearing only a towel and a jersey. I was so enraged at the Sharpie that I used scalding water to scrub it off, and my good friend had been taking care of me while I was blackout drunk but conscious. He was so stressed out by me at this point that he gave me two extra strength Tylenol PMs, and I started to doze off but still not fully having control of my mind yet. My friend was going to sleep, and he started hearing water running, except it wasn't water. I unconsciously decided to start peeing while in the chair out into the bedroom floor! After that, I was out cold, and not just for a couple hours but close to sixteen hours! I woke up at 5:30 p.m. the next night and felt terrible. Here's where the story gets pretty insane, ridiculous, and miraculous.

Over the next few days, I had to piece together everything that happened that night. So here we go...Midnight hit and the ball dropped and I blacked out. I was conscious without memory the *entire* night like a zombie, quite literally. I was convinced by someone that I was a dragon, yes, a *dragon*. I would literally roar and growl all night with low deep growls.

When the party really got started, they all decided to cut off the bottom of the plastic vodka bottle and make a giant funnel. My unconscious self was challenged to drink tank from this makeshift funnel. Well...I was unconscious still, and I drank a *pitcher* full of tank in one go. I could only imagine what damage was being done to my insides. I did go down and lay on this futon for some of the night, while asleep, I peed a good five-foot diameter circle on this futon. Apparently while I was passed out there, I was Sharpied all over my body with green, blue, and yellow Sharpies. Layer upon layer on my face mainly, even on my arms, chest, and back. I fell down outside at one point, tearing down the plants to catch myself so that's where I got some of my bruises. I was carried up the stairs by someone (for whatever reason) and that's where the bruises on my arms came from. I road on the roof of an SUV around the block hanging onto the rails. My best friend was very genuine to me though, and instead of leaving me be, he had others help carry me to his parents' shower and he got some clothes for me and changed me into them. A jersey and some gym shorts. As I sat in the shower after he cleaned me up, I vomited dark brown vomit all over myself. I believe this is why I didn't die that night. Sometime after that, he took the vomit clothes off me and probably turned the shower on me to clean me off (not 100 percent sure though). When I woke up with my own consciousness, I was naked in the towel on the bathroom floor. I was given two Tylenol PMs and didn't know alcohol and Tylenol mixed can shut the liver down, so by the grace and mercy of God, I didn't die that night multiple times.

My twenty-first birthday was debauchery in its fullest. I shot-gunned a 24 oz. beer first. Then friends would just show up with more beer, twelve packs, make your own six packs, and even twenty-four packs. I don't remember much of this night honestly. I just see mercy.

One day, I decided to go on a trip with my friends to visit his mom in Ripley, TN, and then visit his brother who was coming in from active duty in Afghanistan. We got up there to Fort Campbell and my life was such a blur, drinking liquor, and vomiting is what we did the first night. The next night, we went out with his brother, first to his brother's friend's house, then the strip club. The only time I ever went to a strip club. I was just talking and getting to know people at first. Then I asked to have some Crown Royal from the counter. I had a small glass of it, and I knocked it back. Right after, we all went to the strip club, and I was in this nasty tiny strip club with a bouncer in a wheelchair, one stage, and two dancers. I was sitting at the stage, and in a few minutes, I blacked out. I don't even know what happened other than I was taken back to the hotel later and dropped on the bed (still unconscious). Again, I'm so thankful for God's grace to forgive me of my sins.

Another example of not just grace but protection is when I went to my friend's house in Mississippi, way out in the country. We arrived to the gas station close to his house for me to buy a couple of 40s and him to buy some beer and cigarettes. We were coming out of the gas station and someone hit on his girlfriend, so my friend threatens him to stop and the guy doesn't take that lightly but threatened to come to his house after and fight him. We ignored the threat and went back to his house. We start relaxing and I started drinking my first 40 and was still pretty sober. His mom found out about the threat and says we're going over there now to settle this. I sat my 40 down, and we all got in the car and drove over there to the house where they were. We arrived and there were multiple trucks and people waiting, and his mom got out of the car first with a hammer in her hand and tells them to stop. These people are not sober, and I don't know what the rest were on but the big guy there was on either cocaine, PCP, or something along those lines. They jumped her, and my friend and the other friend with us jumped out and started fighting. I look back and wish I had done something to stop it, but I was still dealing with crippling fear. I couldn't move. I couldn't speak. They protected my friend's mom and were getting beat down by the others, and they were literally ganging up and attacking like animals with no conscience. My friend was down on the ground with multiple guys all kicking him in the ribs and head. It was back and forth for a while, and then this big drugged-up man started swinging and with one punch knocked the two front teeth out of my friend's friend. Hit my friend (whose house we were staying at in Mississippi) and then as they were getting in the, car came up and with one punch hit the windshield of my parents' car (which I was driving) and cracked it all the way across, and we left quickly. We found out later that they had hit his mom in the head with that hammer, and she survived. I hate that I was so consumed by fear. If only I had been full of the Holy Spirit and had His courage and power in me at that time, things would have turned out differently, but I believe God protected us even though I couldn't do anything in that horrible experience.

There were so many times where God removed people from my life to protect me, but I still had many things stolen from me before they were removed. I was at my friend's house in Memphis one time, and we were drinking and hanging out by the pool. It wasn't a party as much as it was a get-together, but a few new faces showed up. One girl I asked out after she first arrived, and then later she was drunk and naked just walking around in the middle of the day. She had to leave, and as she was driving away, she immediately went off the road and hit a tree right next to house and everyone outside and around the pool could see it. Her car was totaled and thankfully she survived, but I didn't get to take her on a date...or ever see her again.

I used to work at the Haunted Corn Maze in Cordova, TN, scaring people. It was pretty fun to scare people at that time. I would never do it again though. One night, I and multiple friends all went there and smuggled in some 40s to drink in the corn. We were all drinking and scaring people and having fun. I made a new friend that night who went by Kitty. Kitty and I started dating. Things happened really fast, and before I knew it, I had sinned against her by sleeping with her. I felt so convicted even though I wasn't serving God yet. Shortly after we had done this, in a matter of weeks, I started to notice things about her. She had extreme paranoia and severe schizophrenia. At a certain time each day, her medicine would start wearing off and she would start hallucinating. At first, I still was attracted to her until she started freaking out while with me and my friends. Kitty and I were riding with my friends JT and Liz, and we picked up my friend Cameron. He got in the back seat next to Kitty and me. Kitty said, "My medicine is wearing off." Then she started hallucinating and seeing "pink elephants in the sky," and then she hallucinates when looking at Cameron and says, "Get away from me! He has a frog head!" We were pretty freaked out by that, but she calmed down after that and went back to normal. Another occasion was much worse. Kitty and I were at my friend and his girlfriend's apartment, and she was sitting in my lap and we were smoking a few bowls of weed. Then she started talking to the wall at first, and then she started screaming at the wall. "*Stop it!*" I and my other friends were so freaked out that we didn't know what to do. She said that see saw and heard her Dad yelling at her, but we didn't understand any of that. I broke up with her, and God spoke through me even then with how I worded it, claiming to be a Christian and saying I couldn't be with someone who doesn't believe the same as me and that it wouldn't work. Over a year later, she called me and told me she had turned to God and I still wasn't sober or free of my strongholds yet and just ignored it sadly, but I still pray for her and all my exes to this day.

Spring River trip was another insane story. I was invited to go to Spring River with my best friend and his family. An old friend from middle school, Sarah, went with us. She was one of my exes and my best friend's ex. We got the alcohol before leaving for the trip, and we picked up some thirty-two packs in Arkansas. The first night I drank so much beer but I wasn't mixing it with liquor, so I amazingly *did not* black out and was drunk and still conscious and that was a major feat for me. The next day, we started canoeing, and it was a pretty good day, nothing too crazy…yet. After canoeing and having a few beers, we went to the forty-foot rope swing built into a large tree. The tree had a metal ladder nailed to it at the base, and then when you got higher up the tree, there were rectangle-shaped cut two-by-fours nailed to the tree as a makeshift ladder. To actually swing from the tree, you had to climb almost to the top and have someone else throw you the rope. I didn't do it right at first and tried to swing from the top of the rope and not from the bottom of the rope going out. I couldn't get the momentum I wanted, so I climbed down the rope using only my upper body. When I got to the bottom, I still couldn't get momentum, so I just dropped in the water, which was about twenty-foot deep and decently still at that part of the river. I climbed again and got it right and swung really far on the rope, and that was really fun. After canoeing, we went back to the camp and later decided to go swimming at a different place. We loaded a cooler with beer cans and got down to the area where others were swimming, and there were some other people there with a blowup raft. A snake had gotten into that raft and they were freaking out, so I took the paddle and used it to fling the snake out of the raft and back into the water. From then on, they called me "snake wrangler" Wesley. Hahaha.

After that, we started swimming in the ice-cold spring water, and it was intense but still fun. Sarah was starting to flirt with me and threw a large rock, about eight inches across, at me, and it scathed my leg, because that's the nicest way to show you're interested in someone, I guess. We finished swimming and the night started coming around, and we started drinking more heavily. I was still drinking beer for the most of that night, but once I did get some liquor in my system, it was not good. I don't remember most of that night, so bear with me. The last thing I remember was my best friend's girlfriend's younger brother, Sam, came out in his own vehicle and he was flirting with Sarah. I still liked Sarah, but I was so shy and consumed by crippling fear that I didn't make any moves on her. I got really upset and jealous because I wanted to hook up with Sarah at the time, and once I started getting angry, I was already drunk and the last thing

I remember was punching the solid metal bathhouse door open so hard that it slammed against the wall. I went in the bathhouse and blacked out. I was told later that I was punching the wall and punching the truck we drove up in, and I had no idea. The next morning, I woke up and was covered in bruises, and my fist was extremely swollen, like a balloon blown up. We started drinking again early the next morning and then canoed some more—my best friend, Sarah, and I. We were joking around and we started rocking the canoe, and it tipped over in the water so we were cracking up. We swam the canoe back to shore at the camp.

After that, we went back to the rope swing. We arrived at it and I was tipsy already, and as I was climbing up the shore where the base of the tree is, I slipped and slammed by shin on a branch sticking out of the water. To impress Sarah, I shrugged it off and climbed up the tree. This time I jumped and the rope didn't leave my hand, and I slid forty-foot down with a thin nylon rope ripping into my fingers, and this wound was right in the bend of my middle finger on my already-swollen right hand and it was ripped open. After we left the rope swing and went back to the camp, I was dead tired, my hand would barely move, and my rope burn kept me from being able to close my hand.

We needed to gather some firewood, so to be a "showoff" for Sarah again, I climbed trees and hung from the branches that would break easily and snapped the branches off by hanging from them and then I would break every small branch off the larger branch and then break the larger branch by over hand, throwing it at a tree to snap it in the middle, and I kept doing this to gather large amounts of firewood. After we got the fire going, we started grilling and having a few more beers.

After we ate dinner, we met up with this random family from Arkansas who was also camping there. I remember being conscious there just enough to see this man in his trailer look at his wife and then look at my friend, and he said, "Son, you have my permission." My friend is usually the joking type with quick comebacks, and he was speechless, wide-eyed, and in shock.

They had some liquor there, and I, of course, asked for a couple shots. I was pretty slammed by this point and ready to get some sleep, but the thing was, I blacked out *again*. I wasn't told that I did anything crazy on this night, thankfully.

The last day of the trip, I was sore all over, covered in bruises that I don't know or remember how I even got. My hand is still very swollen from beating the crap out of the bathhouse door, wall, and the truck. We packed everything up and headed back home. We collectively drank 357 cans of beer in three days between me, my friend, and Sarah. I never dated Sarah after that, and I'm sure that it was supposed to happen that way.

At the age of nineteen, I was pretty bad into the party and drug lifestyle, and I went to a friend's apartment to smoke one time and we ended up getting drunk. This was one of the first and only times that I got drunk and was still conscious to remember it. I became friends with the owner of the apartment, who went by D. I was brought out to move some furniture by D, and after the move, I was offered a job on call for other moves. I worked with a guy named Tom, who had thirteen years of moving experience, and he also sold many types of drugs. I became a professional furniture mover from all the insight and tips he taught me from his experience.

Tom was extremely organized with the truck and had every tool necessary to do anything. We moved a good few different places and I gained some serious muscle mass while moving furniture. Tom was involved with some serious drugs and was a thief. He had gotten caught a few times from stores and been kicked out. One night we moved this elderly lady who had pills *everywhere*, on the floor, on her nightstand, in boxes, etc. Tom went through the pills and took whatever he wanted that was of value at all. I don't remember what all kinds specifically, but he gave me a few of them and I took them to my friend's apartment to share them with him. I took about four or five pills including a skeletal muscle relaxer, and I sat back in a chair and was so high off these pills whatever they were and we smoked some weed too, and then I blacked out.

I was at Tom's house one day after a move, and another moving truck pulled up that was driven by two other employees of the same company who had caught the roof of their truck on a tree limb that ripped open the roof of the truck. They said, "We need to take your truck for work," and Tom just laughed and told them to leave.

One of the moves that we did was an office building with all kinds of large heavy furniture, and in the storage room of the offices, there were some miscellaneous items. One of the other movers with us named D decided to steal this blue storage container with a Bluetooth player in it and a few other things, including some pineapple rum and a bottle of Maker's Mark whiskey. They never got caught stealing while on moving jobs, but eventually Tom got raided and I never saw him again.

From the moving jobs, I was given favor and got to work with the owner of the company directly. He was a buff ex-military guy and hardcore. The first day I worked with him, we moved *two* apartments and a storage unit full of furniture in one day, and I held my own.

In between every move, he would allow me to take one small hit of very high-quality Kush. The end of the day came and my arms were locking up after that much heavy lifting, but I managed to push through. Tom was impressed, and I got to do some personal errands for him and even weed eat his yard at his house.

I left a toolbox with some pretty nice tools in it on one of the moving trucks one day, and he never gave it back. I got a call from him a few more times for work, and we moved the houses of some wealthy men. The first was a nightclub owner, and the move required two full trucks to fit everything! This guy was loaded, but stingy. The smell of expensive weed filled the house when we walked in, and he said nothing to us about that. The stairs had a one-inch lip on every step and were L-shaped. He had a dining room set of solid ivory furniture that was extremely heavy. Just one dining room chair was a couple hundred pounds. He also had some luxurious couches that he wanted on the second floor. This man's wife easily had four hundred pairs of shoes, and I filled one bedroom with boxes of shoes! It's sad that people invest so deeply into vanity with temporal things.

The next big move was another loaded and stingy guy. He had a $3,000 bed with four tree trunk-size pillars at each corner and an iron over hanging canopy that sat on the top of the pillars. A ten-foot-tall mirror that we had to hang above his fireplace. He had a top-of-the-line furniture set in his thirteen-year-old daughter's room. Later on that day, his son pulled up in a Denali, with a sound system. A $50,000 car and his son was nineteen, and I was pretty jealous of him at the time. I'm glad I didn't have that kind of money or I wouldn't be who I am today, and I most likely wouldn't be alive. I wasn't ready to responsibly steward money like that yet, and I know now I would have just destroyed myself and others.

I got to do a move with an old military friend of the owner who was not very bright. He was rather careless and broke the leg off a small table, and I knew more than him because of Tom's training me. But he was so full of pride he wouldn't listen. I was full of pride too though and I got pretty mad at this guy, and after that move, I didn't work with him again.

I became good friends with D and started hanging out with him at his house. We were pretty close and would smoke weed together and watch movies. He was a nice guy but had some major anger problems and was abusive to his animals, and this bothered me but I didn't say anything because I was too fearful to speak for myself. I was at his house while his girlfriend was there, and they would fight and she came out with a black eye. I was scared after that but didn't have the courage to do or say anything. They broke up eventually. I couldn't imagine going through that, and I wish I had the courage to do something for her. She was very beautiful and didn't deserve that at all.

I had explosive anger problems of my own, but I would never take it out on people. D eventually got a job at a phone store, and one night decided to steal the store's $1,500 deposit and whatever other electronics he wanted—SD cards, phones, a tablet, and who knows what else. I didn't hear from him much after I moved to Nesbit, MS, with my parents.

He would come out and we would smoke weed together, and the last time I saw D, he stole some hoodies from me. One was an All Shall Perish hoodie that was autographed by the members of Job for a Cowboy, and then he moved into my friend's house out in Mississippi. He used their family and didn't pay rent like he said he would. Then when he decided to move out of there, he had someone pick him up and he stole the most random things from their house—a blanket, some hair clippers, a freakin' lint roller, and all kinds of other things, and then I stopped hanging out with him after that.

I became friends with a couple after meeting them through some friends, JT and Liz. I began going over there all the time to hang out and do drugs, smoke weed, and drink. We got along great, except the problem was that they were a very bad influence on me. I got really into pills with them, especially Xanax and Lortabs.

We would smoke weed all the time and do pills whenever we could. This is when I really abused Xanax the most and developed its side effects. I was being used by them. I would give them things to borrow, and they wouldn't return them. We would do work, and JT would make up some type of excuse to have to leave after he was paid without finishing the job. But not every time. He did finish some jobs.

There was this couple at church who was getting a divorce. The woman's name was Deb, and she had her son Nick with her. I helped her move, and she gave me a nice computer tower with a very nice computer chair for helping them move. Things didn't go well with Deb, and she eventually didn't have anywhere to go. So my parents took her in so she wouldn't be on the street. Deb was an interesting person, and by interesting, I mean she had split personality disorder. I didn't figure this out right away though. Things were pretty calm at first. I started bringing a friend over named B, and B befriended Deb.

One night, JT and Liz came over and had a 2.5-gram blunt rolled up, and we invited Deb to smoke it with us, not knowing if she even smoked, but we knew she was stressed. She was so happy when we did, and we went out back and hotboxed a 2.5-gram blunt and got so stoned we could barely move. Deb started drinking with us and smoking weed with us. This is how we noticed that she had split personality disorder. She would go through my room looking for weed and pills and that was her teenage personality. She had this normal adult personality, which was greatly different from the teenage personality. Then she had a childlike personality and would literally act like a small child at times. It was pretty creepy.

Deb asked me and JT to help her move some things into storage, and so we did. A few weeks later, JT was short on rent, so because I had one of the keys to storage, Satan used JT to get me to be an accomplice in stealing a box of movies that belonged to Nick, Deb's son. We took them to Hastings and sold them to the store for cash. I deeply regret being guilt tripped into doing that despicable act, and it's something I vow to make right no matter how long it takes. Deb didn't find out until she was moving out.

B had become friends with Deb and was doing favors for her. B eventually got pretty bad on Xanax and was so messed up he was slurring his words like he was drunk while at my parents' house, with no sense of judgment just like with alcohol, he tried to seduce Deb and it didn't work. One day after this, Deb received a call from the Memphis police station. She had allowed B to drive her vehicle and he was high on Xanax and had a head-on collision in it and totaled it and got arrested. This was what happened right before Deb moved away from us and found out we had stolen from her.

JT and Liz weren't done with me yet. I got really bad on drugs and fed my addictions to numb my severe emotional and mental pain and anguish, and I borrowed my dad's car and debit card. They influenced me to buy us some food to grill out, so I spent my dad's money for it. I filled up the tank with his card and went out to Lakeland, TN, to a friend's house to smoke weed and hang out. After this, I went on a spending spree for whatever I wanted, which was cigarettes, beer, and food, and before I knew it, I had spent over $200 and my parents' card was declined a bill and they found out what I had done. I came home secretly because I was living a life of deception and lies, but they knew what I had done.

My mom was devastated and crying. I started to recognize what I had become—an addict, a druggie, a liar, a thief, and a deceiver. I felt so bad to see my mom cry, but I still didn't know how to get free. I went through the cabinets in my parents' bathroom and looked for old pills and tried to get high on my mom's antidepressants because JT told me to take them and get effed up. My mom found my phone and went through my messages and found out what I had done, and I wasn't allowed to see JT anymore after that.

There was a friend of mine that I knew from middle school that I somehow got reconnected with named Adam. Adam and I started hanging out in Mississippi at my parents' house and smoking pot together. Adam was having mental issues at the time and was on various different psychotropics. He got by smoking pot, and his mom would help him get it because she didn't know what else to do to help him, and he would have mental episodes when he couldn't have access to marijuana.

One night, I went to help him sneak out to go smoke together. The thing was, his dad was up and watching him.

Adam got in the car and we left, and then we noticed his dad following us. I started to run from him because I was scared and being foolish. I drove like an idiot and wasn't thinking clearly and took and oncoming ramp off a highway and pulled out on the main road in oncoming traffic, so I hopped the curb and the median and went the opposite direction. I lost his dad and then we went to a friend's apartment to smoke together like it was a normal night. After I took Adam home later on, I dropped him off close to his street so he could walk back, and I didn't get caught. But that was the last time I got to see Adam.

As I continued the party lifestyle, God still was with me. One night I was going to my friend's house in University of Memphis area and my car wasn't driving right. This was because it was my first car, and I had no idea how to check or change the fluids and didn't know that I had to. The car was starting to overheat, but I drove very slowly and carefully and made it to my friend's house. We smoked a few bowls and I left, and on the way back, the car really started to overheat and by God's grace, I barely made it back home. The radiator was leaking antifreeze all over the floor of the carport.

Another example of His protection and intervening was when I was with some friends one night and wanted to go to a dubstep rave party in downtown Memphis where a friend of mine was the DJ. We started heading that way, and about fifteen minutes from the venue, the car overheated to the point that we couldn't drive it. We had to pull over and wait about forty-five minutes for the car to cool off to where we could keep driving it, and we started driving and it started shaking (had I continued driving the car, the heads in the engine would have warped and this would have totaled the engine). We pulled into a gas station and filled it with water again and had to wait again for the car to cool down.

What I later found out was my friend at this rave sold MDMA, the purest extract of the main ingredient of ecstasy. A rave party surrounded by drugs and women would not have been a good place for me to be, so God intervened and stopped those plans dead in their tracks. I'm so thankful of the many times I was shown mercy. I was pulled over with alcohol, and the police let me pour out the liquor and let us off with a warning.

CHAPTER 3

DIVINE PROTECTION

Satan hated me my whole life because of whom I would become. Satan tried to set me up for many snares and traps that could take my life before I surrendered to God so that I would die in my sins and be separated from God eternally. Here are the times (that I'm aware of) that I nearly died or was severely injured.

Instance 1: I was moving a fitness gym for a company through a Craigslist ad in Cordova, TN. I loaded a 400 lb. machine on a four-wheel floor dolly and moved it to the truck, and I stepped back to let it slide off the dolly to the floor of the truck. And when I stepped back, the guy behind started letting down the lift gate to let himself down, and he was looking the other way and was unaware of me stepping back. My leg went through the gap, and the machine fell backward directly on top of me and hovered supernaturally about half an inch from my face. I slammed my thigh on the corner of the lift gate and my calf muscle was crushed under the base of the machine, but the top was almost touching my nose. Despite its legs being a V-shape in front of it, the machine didn't splatter my head like a watermelon. I wholeheartedly believe an angel of God was sent to hold it up over my face.

Instance 2: I was in Mississippi at my sister's house at the time and was driving an ATV by myself in this large open field and was drifting at 45 mph right before the tree line at the end of the field, and one of the back tires caught a stump hidden under the tall grass while I was drifting and threw me violently. I rolled through the four- to five-foot tall grass which cushioned me, and I rolled to a stop. As I was laying on the ground, I looked over and the ATV was rolling toward me, and before I knew it, there was one set of tires on my left and one set of tires on my right. I was staring at the bottom of it. I had a bruise and cut on my leg, but that is the only injury I sustained. I crawled out from under the ATV and tried to start it and head back, but the battery was hanging out and wasn't fully connected anymore. I had to push it back to the house.

Back in my freshman year of high school, I was at a friend's apartment and we had my friend Cara with us. We smoked a few small bowls of 10x salvia. (Salvia is a plant that causes hallucinations when smoked, but the hallucinations only last up to ten minutes.) The plant must be extracted by a chemist, and depending on how well they did the extracting of it, the potency was labeled between 5x and 90x. The only difference between the strengths of it was the vivid level of hallucination. They still lasted anywhere from five to ten minutes.

We had a two-foot green bong named the "Green Monster" (after a Suicide Silence song) that we were smoking the 10x salvia out of. My friend said the back of the chair was melting into rainbow colors after he smoked his bowl. I didn't have much visual from my bowl thankfully. Cara didn't want to smoke. After we had smoked, Cara needed to get back home. I briefly dated Cara and was still attracted to her, so when we got there, I tried to make a move. She felt sick all of a sudden. I couldn't do anything, and I believe that was God preventing me from making a terrible mistake. I was disappointed, and I left to head back home. I was on a back road that ran next to Shelby Farms in Cordova, and it was about 1:30 a.m. I was getting tired, and I blacked out at 45 mph behind the wheel in the pouring down rain heading straight for the ninety-degree turn in the road with a giant wooden utility pole at the end of the section of the road. I was instantly woken up right before this crashing head on into the utility pole, and I whipped the wheel to the right. I did a 560-degree turn and hopped a ditch backward, and the car slid in the muddy grass. I was fine and so was my dad's 2000 Camaro that I was driving.

Fully awake and sober, I panicked and tried to pull out of the grass and back onto the road, but it would not work. It was too muddy and the car just spun out and didn't get any traction. I started to slide backward after a couple minutes and slid down into the ditch by the road. I was freaking out now because I knew police would be coming as soon as a car drove past and called them, and I had a two-foot-tall bong and a small candy-cane-shaped tin that said "Jesus" on it, which contained some weed, the slide, and the bowl for the bong. So like a ninja, I ran this "Jesus" tin a few yards away and hid it behind a tree. I went back to the car and had to hide this giant bong, so I used my bare hands to rip the ground up and buried it right next to the car. Sure enough after some time had passed, I saw blue lights pulling up. My adrenaline was pumping, and my heart was racing. They asked, "Are you okay?" and I had just reached someone on the phone, and I said, "Yes, someone is coming to pull me out." Someone I had smoked weed with a few times came out to help pull me out at 3:00 a.m. He arrived with another friend of mine with him, and they tied some straps to the car and pulled me out. I thanked them and got into the car with my heart still racing after it all, and I drove away and then circled back around to retrieve the "Jesus" tin and my bong, which I successfully retrieved with no problems. I cleaned the car off so my parents wouldn't know and then took it home not realizing what all God had done for me that night.

Instance 4: This was some time later when I was older and taking a friend of mine Dustin back to his dad's house way out in Mississippi. I had been up all night, and it was close to 5:00 a.m. and still dark outside. I blacked out driving down Highway 302, and I would have crossed Highway 61 that ran perpendicular to 302 and gone off the road into a dirt hill. But again, I was woken up and managed to stop the car on the edge of Highway 61 parallel with 61.

Instance 5, 6, and 7: The New Year's tank party where I could have died of alcohol poisoning from drinking over two pitchers of tank that night if I hadn't peed and vomited it out of my system.

Riding around the neighborhood on the roof of someone's car. Had I mixed the Tylenol PM with the tank in my system, it would have been fatal.

Instance 8: I was doing a concrete/masonry job through Craigslist. This was my second job with the same person. We were rebuilding the wall of the ditch in the front of someone's front yard near the road, and we had smoked a little bit of weed and had a beer or two before starting work. We had already built the new wall for the ditch and were decorating it with flagstones to make it look nice and a huge rock that was about 100 lb. that I was cementing to the wall broke the seal because the cement had some air behind it and didn't keep suction and fell off the wall while I was right in front of it. I was bending down, so it only hit my shin through the super thick tongue of my Osiris skating shoes, which prevented something much worse. I had a huge gash in my shin even through the tongue of the shoes cushioning, but I'm sure if I hadn't been bending down or had those particular shoes on that it would have gone straight to the bone or even broken my leg. At this same jobsite, I had a wheel barrel full of sand, and I was approaching the edge of the driveway near the ten-foot drop off to the ditch we were working on, and I was too close and almost fell off the edge with the full wheel barrel I was moving and I managed to save myself and the wheel barrel from falling in that moment when my adrenaline kicked in.

Instance 9: I was on Interstate 40 from Nashville heading toward Memphis, and I fell asleep behind the wheel while (sober this time) and was going 70 mph in the fast lane and immediately woke up before hitting the concrete divider.

Instance 10: I was much younger and working with my dad, and loading his truck, I was in the back and had just loaded a tall pallet and he brought in another pallet on a pallet jack to fill in the opening in the back of the truck not knowing I was back there, and it happened so fast I was almost crushed but I jumped wall to wall Super Mario style like a ninja and was sitting on top of the pallets with a foot or two between the top of the pallets and the roof and was unharmed.

Instance 11: I fell asleep again and was going off the highway ramp in Murfreesboro, and I woke up just in time to hit the rumble strips and save it. I stopped my van from flipping off the side of the ramp.

Instance 12: I was doing on call deliveries in my cargo van and hit standing water at 75 mph in the fast lane and almost lost control but saved it.

Instance 13: I was on my way to work and it was winter time. I had no problems all the way to work, and as I was taking my exit, I hit black ice on the off ramp while going 60 mph and turned sideways almost flying off the ramp but I managed to save it right at the edge and stay on the ramp.

Instance 14: I fell asleep behind the wheel again. I woke up just before hitting the semi next to me at 70 mph.

Instance 15: I was going to Marshall County in Mississippi in my dad's Pontiac Vibe with a car loaded full of people to take my friend home. I hadn't been down there that many times yet. It was night time, so it was difficult to see the road to turn on. I was looking for the turn and had some music playing and the people in the car all started yelling telling me to turn at the last second, so I hit the brakes and turned very abruptly and the car almost flipped over and went off the road. God stopped it from flipping and protected us all from rolling at a high speed.

Instance 16: In June of 2017, I was on my way to Memphis from Nashville for work, and it was raining very hard, like to where the windshield wipers were turned all the way up and it was still difficult to see. I was driving too fast honestly, passing people and not being patient. I sped up to pass someone, and then from the slow lane, I sped up again to pass someone else who wouldn't let me over. I switched lanes abruptly directly into standing water and hydroplaned my van at 70-plus mph turned sideways and managed to turn the van back to aiming straight as I flew through the grass median as a ramp with no traction and no way to use the brakes. I hit the guard rail and cables of the oncoming side with the front driver side area of the van where the headlight and driver side hinge of the hood was. I hit the rail at the exact same time as a black semitruck was barreling by. God stopped me from going any further than the rail at that exact moment. I pulled back onto the median immediately after and kept driving! I pulled back onto the shoulder and then back into the fast lane. I went a few miles up to the next exit and pulled off to examine the damage. There were scrapes down the sides of the van, the driver side head light was gone, the driver side mirror was also gone, and the driver side taillight was damaged as well. The front of the van had been crushed in just enough that it wasn't interfering with engine, and it was one to two centimeters from touching the moving serpentine belt. The van was still drivable, so I continued my route and finished it with no driver side headlight or mirror.

Instance 17: I was working at a granite warehouse in Memphis, TN, and this was a cheap granite warehouse where I worked with one other person most of the time. The equipment was pretty worn out and the clamp that attached to the fork lift used to pick up the slabs of granite was starting to have issues. I was standing beside the truck to guide the slab as he loaded it on the truck, and the clamp malfunctioned and dropped this white marble slab. I jumped out of the way as it hit the truck flat bed and fell over my way and shattered on the floor.

Instance 18: I was involved in a head-on collision and I miraculously survived.

Instance 19: The suicide attempt on the balcony interrupted.

Instance 20: I was driving for my job on my way back from Clarksville back to Nashville after my route. It had snowed very heavily for a couple of days and the interstate had thick snow on it. Everyone was driving about 45 mph except for semis, and I started sliding and almost went off the road but managed to stop the sliding in time to not go off the road where a drop-off was.

Instance 21: I was driving home to visit my family and was in the fast lane at 80 mph, and this flatbed semitruck came over in my lane without any notice because someone had come into their lane suddenly and they were avoiding being hit from the right side. I slammed on the breaks and barely avoided crashing into the back of the truck.

Instance 22: I was doing a delivery to Knoxville. I hit some black ice at 70-plus mph and almost lost control, but I managed to save it.

Instance 23: I had an impatient driver pull off from the dock with me in the back of the truck. (More about this story later.)

Instance 24: Head-on collision in July of 2017 that I'll explain more on later.

Some people deny the existence of angels and claim that super-natural occurrences do not happen today. I *know* that angels do exist and do as they are commanded by God and by humans and that God still works supernaturally today to intervene in our lives when things are going wrong or we are facing imminent danger.

CHAPTER 4

BROKEN

My breaking point was when I purposefully would buy 13 percent alcohol content wine and drink the bottle to myself only to get a buzz. That's when I woke up from the nightmare of alcoholism and realized how pointless that lifestyle was and that what I was chasing could never satisfy me. I just wanted to have "fun," but the end result was nothing but agony. I was finally getting broken down to the point of no return, and I was still living for myself and felt horrible and unfulfilled.

I was arrested multiple times in different counties for different offenses and illegal activity. God would wreck my plans before I could wreck myself. I was given so many warnings, and I can look back and see all the times God showed me grace and mercy with the law. I had times when I would be drunk driving and would black out at the wheel, and God would immediately wake me up before I would crash. This happened so many times, and I had a few accidents involving others because I would fall asleep while driving and those were minor and no one was hurt. I'm so thankful for His protection even when I lived in opposition to His laws and statutes and the laws of the land.

I got a job at a car wash, and one night, I was drinking and had two forty-ounce beers and a mixed drink with Everclear. I woke up late around twelve noon and rushed straight there and had to relay a message to the general manager, and though I was sober, the alcohol was strong on my breath from the night before and he thought I was drunk and I lost the job. I was shown grace and was blessed with a job at FedEx because the staffing agency didn't drug test me. I liked the job and got really good at what I did there and was quickly promoted to loading the Forest City truck there with three others because it had very fast moving volume. I learned many different positions in the warehouse and was a hard worker. I gave some of my first paycheck to my parents, but eventually I started coming up with excuses to keep all the money and go spend it on my friends to get drunk and high. God doesn't like selfish motives, so to make me lose the job, FedEx dropped the whole staffing agency. I and about sixty others lost our jobs.

After that, God wouldn't allow me to have a job because that money would be spent on destruction of myself and others. Being unemployed for so long, I was running out of options, and I started scrapping metal with a friend. There is legal and illegal scrapping. We started out legally and made some decent money, and then we started thinking about where we could find places that produced metal daily and we started asking around to find places like that. We started finding places and were making really good money from it, and we would go at nighttime and we never got caught at one place. And at another, we were run off by a warehouse worker, so we quickly climbed out of the dumpster and sped off.

My dad told me about a place he had done deliveries to in Hernando, Mississippi, called Spiral Manufacturing that produced scrap metal. We went there one night to see what they had, and we started loading the truck. We had it fully loaded and were tying it down when the owner pulled up around 4:00 a.m. and he called the police on us and then confronted us. We didn't fully understand the laws of scrapping metal, and we thought, "It's better to ask forgiveness than permission." (Which is a very stupid phrase.)

We told him we didn't understand the laws and didn't know there was a contract on their dumpster, so we, being fueled by adrenaline, put it all back before police arrived and asked forgiveness. The police arrived and the man decided to press charges despite us putting all the scrap metal back in the dumpster.

The police searched my friend's truck we were in, and I was sitting in the back of the cop car and remembered the hydrocodone pills I had in there and my heart sank. I was so scared, but by God's mercy, they didn't find the pills. They did, however, find our marijuana and the small one hitter we had in there, so I got a paraphernalia charge later on.

We got arrested and taken to jail in Hernando, MS. I was so full of rage and hatred toward the man who pressed charges that I yelled and screamed out my violent thoughts toward him that night in my cell. My cell mate was a smooth talker and seemed to be a nice person. He told me he was in jail because he left the fireplace going after his roommate left for work and the place burned down by accident. I didn't have any problems while I was there. I was bonded out by my parents the next day and put on probation for six months.

My new computer at that time crashed, and I lost 130 gigabytes of metal and horrible movies.

During my first court date, I wasn't allowed to bring my phone in the building, and I was dropped off so I hid the phone in the bushes. My phone got stolen because someone overheard me say that I hid it in the bushes, and I lost nine gigs of more horrible music and all my drug contacts and dealers.

I went back to the party life as usual, but this time, God was drawing me. He used people, music, movies, and different circumstances to speak to me. I was becoming an agnostic and choosing to not care anymore. It was the coldest time of my life, devoid of hope and filled with sorrow. Thankfully, God used a guy named Yuri at the Germantown library to befriend me and lead me back to God. I didn't see Yuri very much, and then he was sent off to rehab by his parents and I lost contact with him.

I was at a friend's house and a book on his bedroom floor read *Overcoming Tough Times with God*, but I still didn't believe yet. I was realizing the value of the eternal soul and how unimportant money and material things were. I was given $20 from my good friend Alstone just because he was a good friend to me. I spent most of it and was down to $1, and I gave it to a homeless man simply because he needed it more than me. That's when God really turned toward me because my heart was changing. John 3:16–17 says, "God so loved the world that *He gave*…His only Son that whoever believes in Him would not perish but have everlasting life, God didn't send His Son to condemn the world but that through Him they might be saved."

I kept drinking even still, but without being able to do drugs because of probation, I had more sober moments of realization and how my life was heading toward destruction. I was over $5,000 in debt to the state, probation, bail bonds, and my parents, and at this point, I was done. I was depressed, suicidal, and hearing demonic voices telling me horrible violent and perverse things and filling my head all day every day. I would drown myself in alcohol and video games to either numb or escape the pain. I had been unemployed for two-and-a-half years. I was ready to end it all and I didn't care anymore.

On the night of August 7, 2012, at the age of twenty-one, I was so depressed and felt hopeless. I had just drunk a couple of beers and felt dead inside. The reality of it all overwhelmed me, and I was being crushed beneath the weight of fear, shame, guilt, regret, pain, suffering, depression, self-hatred, and unforgiveness. I didn't know what else to do, and I wanted to escape this hellish reality, so I broke and went on the balcony and my mind was racing and hopelessness was devouring me. I was alone and the others had left, and while they were gone, I made the decision to jump off the third story balcony of my friend's apartment. There I stood on the balcony and the second the thought crossed my mind my dad's phone rang. I had my dad's phone on me that day because mine was stolen. It was my sister Amanda calling to get in touch with my dad. I answered and She asked me how I was doing and I was completely honest, broken, I didn't care at all and I told her that I felt hopeless. She told me all the things God was doing in her life and encouraged me. She told me about how she fell off a horse at 30 mph and miraculously didn't get hurt at all. How her boyfriend won the $500 max prize at a Guitar Center drawing after praying over the papers to move around as necessary so they could buy a new microphone for their worship music they were recording. She told me to "*leave no stone unturned* in my life" and to trust that God could turn my life around and save me.

She encouraged me for twenty minutes, and she's the reason I'm alive today, all because she listened to God the moment He spoke to her. I hung up with her and felt something I had never felt before: hope. Ready for a change and willing to keep pressing on, I said, "God, if you're real, I give you everything. I'm done and I don't want to live anymore, so I give you everything."

CHAPTER 5

REBIRTH

Everything laid out before God, and I wasn't turning back. I went back to church after months of not going because I got drunk and partied every Saturday and couldn't wake up on time to go and my priorities were not to go. I put all the money I had in the offering bucket, and it was $1.47 but it was everything I had. I was on the front row on my knees praying and giving God everything. Tears were streaming, and I was asking forgiveness for all my sins and repenting. God heard my prayer, and the Holy Spirit came and filled me. God healed my brain cells, memory, liver, lungs, and all my internal organs. My body was restored to brand-new instantly. All the damage I had done through years of excessive drug abuse, excessive drinking, and a destructive reckless lifestyle was undone in a single moment. I used to zone out midsentence and forget what I was even saying. My vocabulary was shot. I couldn't even remember common words anymore. I had horrible short-term memory. I had this incredibly thick haze over my mind, and *boom!* Crystal clear in a split second! Once I was filled, I had profound wisdom and understanding of things like I had never experienced before! I was given a second chance. I walked up to a man at the church named Ken, and I apologized to him. Months ago when I had just smoked a ton of pot with some friends, we all came to church for a Wednesday night service and they went upstairs, but I was in the bathroom and Ken smelled the marijuana on us and confronted us and was afraid. I ran and jumped the fence and then later came back and took my parents' car and left. I knew I needed to apologize to Ken for my actions so that's what I did, and he was shocked and saw a change in me.

I started going to church every chance I could get. I was healed mentally and physically, but emotionally and spiritually was going to take some process. I still had demonic thoughts because of the dark and horrible content of music, movies, and pornography I had opened doors to in my life about violence, perversion, pedophilia, incest, rape, greed, depression, condemnation, self-hatred, fear, and lust, but I was no longer spiritually dead. I recognized the thoughts were from the enemy and his demons, and I knew I needed to pray again and I was at home and I asked my parents to pray for me and they lead me in the Sinner's Prayer. I prayed the Sinner's Prayer with true sincerity and with my parents praying over me, and all the voices stopped! No more full sentences about killing myself and others and other perversions of all kinds. I was free from years of demonic attacks! I knew what to do now, and every time I would hear something tempting me to sin, I would pray, "I bind and rebuke you spirit. I am covered in the blood of the Lamb and a new creation in Christ!"

Three days later, my dad called and told me he found a job for me! I went to an interview and filled out my application, turned it in, and the door behind me opened. I was greeted by the owner of the Memphis branch of Crosstown Couriers. He said, "Hi, I'm Scott. You will be delivering Avon. It pays this much. You will work on these days, you will need a cargo van, and you have training the seventeenth." That is what an open door from God looks like! The job fell in my lap and was prepared by God for me.

I had some time before I would start the job with Crosstown Couriers, and I found some ads on Craigslist for roofing jobs. I called the ad and got the job. I and my friend Jimmie both went to the job site and started working for a guy named Danny. Danny had thirty-plus years of roofing experience, so he trained us and I was natural at it and enjoyed it. I didn't have the right shoes for that job and slipped and almost fell off the roof, but I managed to catch myself. Danny had us keep working for him after the first job. We got a bigger job at an apartment complex. We got to roof an apartment building and I wasn't very strong yet in my legs to carry the seventy- to eighty-pound roofing shingle bundles on my shoulder up the ladder. I brought a small flat pillow to act as a saddle, and Jimmie would put the bundles on my shoulder until I was strong enough to pick a bundle up for myself.

We carried about 3,000 lb. of shingles to the roof up three flights of stairs and then a small ladder from the third floor to the roof. After we finished the job at one building, we were called back to do the second building. This time it was one ladder from the ground up two stories to the roof. This took about a week to get finished, and I carried 160 bundles up that week and really got the hang of it and made some money toward my debts.

During the week of that roofing job, I wanted to hang out with my friend Shawn, so I picked him up, picked up a make-your-own six-pack of beer and a small bottle of Fireball whiskey, and went back to Mississippi to my parents' house. We were about to open the beer, and he got a call from his roommate Courtney saying that she was going to be coming home early that night and needed the key to get in her apartment. We took the alcohol with us and went back to Midtown Memphis to her apartment and she wasn't home yet, so we went in and had a beer while waiting on her. I wanted to leave and leave the keys for her in an anonymous safe place. I asked Courtney if I could leave them above the door, on the back balcony at the top of the staircase, and many other places, and she refused every time saying that it wouldn't be safe. After we sat in the apartment for a while, she called Shawn and said she was going to her friend Breezy's house and to take the keys there and leave them for her.

We went to Breezy's house and were sitting outside, and I wanted to leave the keys and get going back to my parents with Shawn to hang out and have a few beers. Breezy came out and came up to the car and invited us inside, so we went inside and that's where I met Lauren. Lauren was Breezy's older sister, and she was attracted to me and as soon as the conversation went in the direction to where I said, "I surrendered my life to God," Lauren came and sat next to me and took my phone and put her number in it. She was very beautiful, and God wanted me to be with her. Every possible thing that could have prevented me from meeting her could not stop what God ordained.

I started dating Lauren almost immediately. She didn't have a vehicle, so I met her for ice cream at Baskin Robbins, and we talked for a while and immediately connected. We connected so well that we went back to her apartment and kept talking, and we talked for four hours nonstop. I stayed the night there. She had an incredible testimony. She was an atheist before turning to God. She had a rough life and was turning to drug use to cope, and God miraculously saved her from over dosing. This experience led her to believe in Him. I kept going back to Lauren's apartment every chance I could get to keep spending time with her and getting to know her. We were like lovebirds, and I made the mistake of almost going too far with her while making out. I could have, but the Holy Spirit empowered me to stop myself. Afterward, she said, "I know the spirit of God lives in you to be able to stop." I didn't use wisdom with my relationship with her and acted too quickly, and then she became really busy and so did I. I didn't keep trying to communicate because I didn't want to mess anything up, but I did mess things up. I stopped hearing from her, and I didn't have the wisdom I needed to handle the relationship in a godly way. She stopped talking to me, and I was too busy to keep communication going with her. This devastated me, but I was still dealing with shame, fear, guilt, and depression still, on top of drinking and smoking. Even though I was saved, I didn't know how to fix my mistakes.

The job with Danny was over with and I never heard from him again because he had gotten back on heavy drugs. A few days before the training for Crosstown Couriers, I got a letter saying my driver's license was suspended for six months due to the paraphernalia charge that I got because I was driving my friend's truck at the time of arrest for scrapping metal in Hernando. I panicked and worried at first but then decided to hit my knees to the floor and surrender the outcome to God. I was making decent money roofing, but the job had ended. Training day at Crosstown was closing in. I still had no solution, but I kept trusting God.

My mom gave me the idea to pay my friends to drive for me, and Crosstown allowed me! I went in and learned the scanner and what the job entailed. I was so used to everything going wrong, but training went smoothly. My parents rented me a cargo van to start out work, so I hired a few different friends to drive for me and got the hang of the route. A few weeks of working and my parents and I could no longer afford to rent a cargo van. We had a few days until the last day before we could afford to rent it again, so we went out to a car lot in Millington in my dad's '96 T-Top Camaro and found a van that was kind of janky and run-down but did run. We offered to even trade the Camaro for the cargo van, and the guys said they have too many vehicles and don't need any more so we were refused the sale.

We didn't know what to do, so we kept praying and having faith. The day before we couldn't rent it again, my dad got a call that after noon from Hill Stop Motors saying they had multiple new cargo vans coming in!

We went up there, and they worked out a deal with us to get one that day! It was ninety-six degrees outside that day, so because of the heat, the guy there was able to remove most of the decals! I got a 2006 Ford Econoline state-maintained Millington Telephone van that was in great condition! We traded in the Camaro and had a couple other $500 down payments to make on it but were able to drive home in my new cargo van! I started work with my new van and was able to help my friends out with work, but I wasn't wise with finances yet and couldn't pay them what I said I could at first. I was still drinking beer and smoking weed because I didn't know any better yet. I was getting the hang of the deliveries and getting used to talking to people through this job by having to knock on women's doors who were the Avon distributors.

Delivering Avon was a great job, and I was able to start paying some debt off. But the second court date for scrapping metal was coming up, and I was going to need a lawyer. My friend missed his first court date, so he had a warrant put out for his arrest, and he turned himself in to avoid further trouble. His girlfriend and I were teaming up to get a lawyer and she found a great one, but we didn't know how we were going to pay the retainer fee and get him to take our case.

One day, my dad called me and said that FedEx had some scrap metal we could have that they were throwing out and he had asked about. So one day, we went to FedEx in my dad's truck, and they were throwing away a set of sixty-foot rollers, a broken pallet jack, and a couple huge metal fans. We struggled to get the rollers out of the dumpster but had the idea to tie a strap around them and use the truck to pull them out which actually worked. We had all the scrap metal loaded up and took it back home. My friend Shawn and I worked to break down all the rollers and I was allowed to use my friend's truck while he was in jail from turning himself in to take the scrap up to the scrap yard. We drove up on the scales and dropped it all off, and it turned out being 1,400 lb. and we were paid $140.00 for it all. A hundredfold blessing from the $1.47 that I had given at church a few weeks earlier.

I set aside $14 for offering, used some for gas, and saved the rest for a retainer fee for the lawyer. My friend's girlfriend and I went together to the lawyer's office and told him what our case was. We told him we didn't have enough for his retainer fee but he told us to give him what we could afford and he would help us out. We had together between us $487 and God gave us favor, and he took our case despite usually having a $1,500 retainer fee. The court date came up and our lawyer got us off the hook, and we only had to pay court costs. I was about to get off probation and wasn't free from addiction yet, and I started to make some very stupid decisions.

CHAPTER 6

RETURN TO MY VOMIT

One night, I met up with my friend in Mississippi and were headed back to his friend's house in Memphis in a pretty bad area, but I didn't know this yet. I was following my friend so that he could lead because my license was still suspended, and he turned left at a light. I went to go turn at the light, and this car was speeding down the road. So as I was turning, this car barely missed me because I slammed the gas pedal to the floor and shot out from in front of him in seconds, and I was shaken up after this but kept driving. A cop pulled up behind me and pulled me over. He said he pulled me over for reckless driving when the other car almost hit me and he didn't see it. He ran my license and saw that it was suspended, so I told him I was going to my friend's house just up the road. God showed me grace, and the officer gave me a misdemeanor ticket but let me go!

I got to the house just a couple blocks away and had no idea I was at a trap house. I stayed the night there, and in my limited understanding thought that I could just move in and offer to pay rent so I could save money on gas because it was closer to get to and from work. That was absolute folly to think that way. I stayed there a couple of nights, and everyone was doing drugs, weed, spice, and even meth (that I found out about later). I only smoked pot while I was there and never did anything harder.

I woke up one of the mornings I was there and went out to the van, and the driver side mirror had been knocked off by someone reckless driving on the street. I was pretty upset about this and realized I didn't want to be there at all. So I moved out and was never going back over there again.

I was with my friend Mikey one day going to do my Millington route for Avon and I was driving at first to go get some breakfast at Sonic and then to the first house and then let him drive the rest of the day. We were in a neighborhood and made a U-turn and turned back on to the main road, and Mikey noticed a cop car that had passed us turned around and was about to come pull us over. The cop pulled us over, and I incriminated myself by showing him the ticket for driving on a suspended license. He arrested me and took me to jail and let Mikey take my van, which was loaded with Avon and the fact that it wasn't impounded saved thousands of dollars. Mikey ran part of my route while I was in jail until he could reach my dad and get me bailed out. While I was in the detaining cell, I was in there with another guy, so thinking that God had a reason for this, I shared my testimony with the man and encouraged him that God could do the same things for him and restore his life. I was in jail for a couple of hours and was bailed out, and Mikey came and picked me up. I called my lawyer and let him know what happened, and God gave us favor with him and he said there was no need to jump through any more hoops and that I just needed to keep paying off my court costs and fees.

There was a purpose in me getting pulled over. More than just witnessing to that man, I needed to stop drinking and smoking weed, and God was giving me a wakeup call.

One morning, Jimmie and I were loaded up with Avon, and we left the warehouse and got a flat tire while still in the parking lot. We prayed and asked God to provide a way out of this, and after just a few minutes, a door opened from one of the warehouses and a man with a handheld air compressor came out and walked over to us and helped us air the tire, which had come off the rim, and it aired right back up and was ready to go.

The warehouses around us all had blacked out windows and solid metal doors, so no one could see us. We asked him how he knew to help us, and he just simply pointed his finger "up" and then went back to door he came out of. We were given many opportunities for extra work with other routes and helping out with other problems at work when things went wrong, and after a few months of work, a couple thousand dollars of probation, bail bonds, court costs, and drug test fees were paid off! As my two final paychecks came in to finish off the debt, Avon switched couriers and the door closed, and everyone lost their routes.

My final week, I got called to come fill out paperwork. I went up to the office, and Crosstown hired me directly and cut out the middle man, Fusion Logistics, for the Avon route. Four or five months went by and I got little to no on-call work.

During that time, God gave me a job at a granite warehouse to provide my needs. I worked with a nice guy who was schizophrenic. We got along great, and God gave me the opportunity to pray for him. One day at the warehouse, the clamp was faulty and was falling apart, and it malfunctioned and a marble slab fell and almost killed me. The slab fell and I jumped out of the way as it crashed into the floor shattering into pieces. This job was short lived, but I was thankful it provided my needs in that time. God was taking care of me despite my occasional drinking and smoking.

The granite warehouse was done, and I started looking for other ways to make money. I got a call from my church, and Ken needed help from me to do some work around the church. I worked with him a week or so and taped off some things for painting to be done. After that job, I found an odd job from Craigslist to move some furniture. I called and they accepted me, so my friend Jimmie and I drove out there. It ended up being a huge job that took eleven hours total. This was a blessing for both of us, but what was really awesome was the woman was moving to Hawaii. The truck was too full, so she gave away many things. Washers and dryers and other nice things to her neighbors, and we were given a sectional couch, a Lay-Z-Boy recliner, a large red rug, and a few other miscellaneous items for free!

Jimmie and I split up what we were given, and I had a very nice sectional couch. I didn't have a place to store it, so my parents wanted to buy it from me. I agreed and they told me to take $1,500 off my debt to them. What a blessing! That was $5,073 of debt total that was paid off by that time!

There was a nice couple at church named David and Leah. I was called to help them move because I had a cargo van and could help. I helped them move to their new place and found out they didn't have a bed at all and were sleeping on egg crates only on the floor. I had an extra mattress in my room, a couch I didn't need, and a TV I didn't use anymore. I offered it to them because I knew they needed it more than me and I wanted to bless them. I went and picked it up with their sons riding with me to help. We loaded it all up and took it to their new place that same night. My pastor paid me $160 for all I did for them and that was such a blessing to be a part of that.

I got another job from Craigslist doing masonry and cement work with a guy named Danny. I worked a few jobs with him, and we would smoke pot and drink a little while on the job. We finished a job one day and went to go buy some pot. I bought $20 worth of pot and a six-pack of beer and then we went back to his sister's apartment. While sitting in the parking lot in broad daylight, we rolled up a blunt and smoked it while we had a few beers. We were sitting there in a smoke-filled van, and I felt this prompt in my spirit that we needed to leave. I pulled out of the lot and pulled down further into the apartments toward his sister's place. Right as I pulled out of the lot, we were in a police officer pulled in behind us and started slowly following us. I drove up to his sister's apartment and parked the van, and the cop put his lights on after that and walked up to my window. I rolled my window down, and he said, "Who are you and what are you doing here?" "If you tell me the truth, I'll let you go." I responded, "We just finished work, and I am dropping my boss off at his sister's apartment where he is staying." The officer said, "Okay, I believe you. Now what are we going to do about the marijuana?" I said, "I'll give it to you and you can destroy it right now." He let me grind it into the ground and put it down the drain in the parking lot.

He then said, "We still have to go through the motions." He put me in the back of his car uncuffed, and I felt so stupid. I prayed, "God, I'm so sorry and I get it."

CHAPTER 7

DISCIPLESHIP

The very next day following sitting in the back of the cop car at Danny's sister's apartment, I was told about a discipleship class through my church that would last two weeks. I asked Danny if he would like to go too, and he said he would. We went to church, and it was off to Pegram, TN, to a small camp. I grew exponentially while I was there. Pastor Pate was our teacher most of the time we were there. We had a full schedule of learning about the Bible, prayer, intercession, meditation, and tons of great subjects. There were seven of us there total, and we had a great time growing in God. One day, I called my friend Mikey to come out and be a part of it with me. He reluctantly agreed, and the next day, Pastor Pate drove back to Memphis and picked Mikey up and brought him out to Pegram where we were. We found out that this call saved Mikey's life because a guy he owed money to had come that very night and fired shots into his bedroom window right where he would have been sleeping.

Cody shared his testimony, and it was powerful and he didn't finish sharing it for two-and-a-half hours. His story made Mikey break down and receive Christ, rededicating his life, and we embraced with tears and I was so proud of him for making that decision.

One of the days while there, they were messing around, and while I was talking to Pastor Eric about what to do about my friend Matt who didn't believe in God, I was interrupted by Mikey and he got me to come outside. He came up behind me and smashed a cupcake in my eye, and it was all in good fun but I still had some serious anger problems in my heart. I internalized it in front of them and didn't let them see me snap, but I wiped the cupcake off and slammed it to the ground and walked back to my room. I was so upset that a conversation about how to witness to one of my best friends Matt was cut short, and I was in the shower that night and broke down. I felt like I blacked out with rage and anger, and I had a vision of myself scraping my skin off with a rusty knife. I fell to my knees in the shower, so weary from being consumed by anger so deep that I didn't know how to get free from. I prayed and made it through the surfacing rage from my heart.

During the prayer lessons, we started practicing praying for those who we could think of and we prayed for my friend Joe who was in prison at the time. We prayed for many others, and I had severe back pain because I slouched all the time growing up and had terrible posture because I didn't know any better. I also had done so much manual labor, and that was catching up to me as well. I asked for prayer for my back and they prayed for me, and I felt the immense heat from underneath their hands from the Holy Spirit fire. My youth pastor Brittany said, "Bend over and test it out." I bent down and the second I did I felt my spine straighten and my back was completely healed instantly!

Another day we were there we all helped with Mission 615 and helped set up tables and chairs for the homeless outreach event. Being a part of that changed me forever. God used that two weeks to build a strong foundation for me. I was given words from my pastor that God was consolidating all that I had learned growing up and combining it with all the new things I had learned. Danny really grew closer to God through this discipleship class as well. We had a great time doing fun things as well as learning and growing deeper in God. I'm so thankful I didn't go to jail right before we left, and I know God intervened to make sure that I would get to go to that discipleship class because I needed it.

I was looking for where to go next and I called Art Institute and was accepted! I wasn't out of the woods yet though. I still struggled with smoking weed and drinking. A couple months went by while I lived at home with my parents and spent time reading the Bible daily. I loved Proverbs and wisdom. I still listened to a few different secular artists and was playing League of Legends all the time in between reading God's Word. I went on a spree and sought out *all* the Christian metal artists I could find and made a huge list. I knew I needed to listen to mainly Christian music, but I still loved the sound of many secular artists as well. I was following through with the process to get into school, and I was given a move in date of September 29, 2013. I moved to Hermitage, TN, to attend the Art Institute for Graphic Design. Before the moving day, I called Tim, the owner of Crosstown in Nashville, about a job. He arranged for me to start when I got there!

It was the end of September when God called me to Nashville, TN, to attend The Art Institute for Graphic Design. I loaded up my cargo van with my belongings, and it was off to Nashville. I knew that it was time to move away from Memphis and that I wouldn't be able to overcome my struggles with drugs and alcohol addiction if I stayed in the Memphis area. The temptation in Memphis was too strong, and I had already fallen back into drinking and smoking weed a handful of times.

Before I left, I prayed "break my heart for what breaks Yours." I moved to a little town just East of Nashville called Hermitage. When I arrived at the student housing in the Colonnade Apartments, Yahweh had already begun answering that prayer. The apartment was a midsize two-bedroom with four students, two per bedroom. My roommate was easy to get along with, and we had no problems or arguments the whole time I was there. He kept to himself, and we had small talk here and there. We became acquaintances during my stay. The other two roommates weren't home yet, and I didn't know what to expect.

When the other two roommates across from us arrived, I knew that I was going to have a challenging time living with them because they were both effeminate homosexual men. I struggled with that right away because I had the most passionate hatred for homosexuality because of being molested at the age of twelve, but YHWH was answering my prayer to "break my heart for what breaks yours" by showing me firsthand that He loves homosexuals and He shed His blood and died to be in relationship with them too. I knew as soon as I met them that my time here was not going to be easy or pleasant.

In Memphis, right before I lost my job delivering Avon, I was hired on to Crosstown Couriers directly as an employee, so when Avon switched courier companies and dropped Crosstown temp drivers, I still had a job, sort of. I didn't realize at that time what YHWH had in store for income for me, but I quickly followed up with Crosstown Couriers in Nashville at their corporate office as soon as I got housing squared away. I had only briefly met the owner of Crosstown while working back in Memphis, but that was my lead and it was going to have to work.

After a quick phone call to the owner of Crosstown, Tim, I was headed in for an interview and to fill out paperwork. Everything was going great with the interview process, but I had a rude awakening that I didn't expect would catch up to me.

Everything was going smoothly with the interview process, and when it seemed like I had the job and was about to get a start date, I was told to go to Concentra for my drug test. Before I moved, I wasn't able to shake smoking pot yet, and I had just smoked the weekend before with some friends and I was freaking out with fear. "What if I messed up my only shot at getting this job? What have I done?" The questions were racing through my mind, and I felt so ashamed. Reality was setting in, and I didn't think I was going to get the job. Despite all this, I had to remember how YHWH had brought me this far. I prayed, "God, I'm so sorry I messed up and smoked even when I knew better. If it's your will, I ask that I can pass this drug test because I really need this job..." I finished taking the drug test and turned it in. I didn't know what to expect and a couple of weeks went by.

One day, I received a call from Tim at Crosstown. I humbly answered in fear. I was prepared for the worst, but Tim said, "Your paperwork is finished and drug test came back..." (I felt weighed down with anticipation). "Good news! You got the job and start Monday." I broke down in tears and thanked YHWH for being merciful and gracious to me despite my failures and was so blown away at His goodness, especially because I didn't believe I was worthy of it.

CHAPTER 8

OFF TO SCHOOL

New beginning

It was time to start Art Institute, and I arrived early for my first day of class. I parked my '06 cargo van and walked up to the massive front of the building and used my student ID to get inside. I didn't know anyone and was the "new kid" and a freshman. Art school was actually enjoyable, and my teachers were all nice and easygoing. Students didn't mess with me, and I kept to myself most of the time because I was still ruled by shame and fear. I was hopeful to share Jesus with the students and teachers but was still very much in bondage to the things of my past and was afraid to talk much. Shortly after I started school, I was asked by a random girl from one of my classes if I wanted to be friends with benefits to which I declined.

I started my job for Crosstown and started getting sent orders, so I plugged in the addresses and was thrown right into the deep end of the on-call delivery world of Nashville, TN. Oblivious to the roads and city, I relied on the GPS completely to get around and complete every delivery. Delivering anything and everything, big and small, everywhere.

I had my classes and job set up and going well and the next step was finding a home church. I felt lead to go to Friendship World Outreach in White House, TN, about thirty-five minutes northwest of Hermitage. This church was associated with the church I grew up in Memphis, Christian Heritage Church. I arrived at this small church building in White House and went inside the front glass double doors. I had only met a couple of the people that attended there, but they accepted me with open arms and welcomed me. It was a great atmosphere, and I felt loved and valued right away. After a couple of weeks, I was invited out to serve at Mission 615. Mission 615 was an inner-city kids and homeless outreach. Every Saturday FWO (Friendship World Outreach) would send five school buses to various locations in Nashville to pick up homeless people and bring them back to their little church in Pegram, TN, where I attended discipleship school. The church service consisted of a contemporary worship set, a sermon, and then a free meal and clothing closet. The volunteers would set up and tear down a couple hundred chairs and a few tables for the meal and the racks for the clothing closet every week. I jumped right on board and got involved. I would carry chairs, tables, clean, etc., and do whatever needed to be done. Little did I know this was going to be one of the most personally transforming experiences of my life.

The first few months were hectic and exhausting but very productive. I would finish up my class and call dispatch to tell them I was available and rarely would I ever refuse a job. I enjoyed what I was doing and was becoming better and better at it. I was a workaholic and would work myself too much, but I was paying about $345 a month toward my student loans while I attended school and getting ahead on my debt so it was worth it to me.

Mission 615 was only in Pegram a few weeks when I first began volunteering and then YHWH opened a door for them to move to Nashville and He used me and my friend Mikey to help them. Before I moved away from Memphis I was at Mikey's house and we were asked if we could come out to Pegram and help Mission 615 move to their new location. I didn't have the gas needed to get there and my van wasn't running at the best capacity but Mikey and I headed out anyway. We drove from Marshall County Mississippi all the way to one mile before the Pegram, TN, exit on a quarter tank of gas and faith. Nearly two hundred miles! It was a miracle! We broke down on the side of the interstate just before the exit we needed to get to not because of low fuel but because the battery went out. We called Cody who was one of the leaders over Mission 615 and told him what was going on. He drove to meet us and we tried a few different things but couldn't get the van to start. We decided we would hook up jumper cables from each vehicle and slowly drive to the church. We creeped along so as to not unhook the jumper cables and it actually worked. We arrived at the church safely and realized Cody, Mikey, and I were the only ones there to move all the tables and chairs. We singlehandedly loaded it all up into the truck and left for the new location in Nashville. We pulled up to the new location and thankfully a few others were there to help unload the truck until we finished the job. We road back with Cody in the truck to Pegram, and when we arrived, we still had to figure out what to do about my van. We were blessed randomly with the money needed to get a new battery, and Cody knew a great mechanic in the area who helped us out. YHWH provided our every need because of His faithfulness.

I would have classes and work most days, and every weekend, I would serve at Mission 615 and I loved it. I was humbled every time I would see these kids from low-income neighborhoods and homeless learning about who Jesus was.

I started with setting up and tearing down the stage, the speakers, lights, tables, chairs, etc., every week. I would fill whatever spot needed to be filled and eventually moved on to helping set up and tear down sound equipment, running the sound board, and running the media on the computer for the kids' service and adult service. I had my struggles, but being a part of this and hearing all the stories that caused people to get into their situations taught me to be so thankful for all that I had.

CHAPTER 9

RESCUER

School, work, church, and Mission 615 were going great for a while but a schedule that hectic eventually began to burn me out. I didn't have much friends from school and spent most of my time with my church family, but as I grew less afraid of people, I would make some silly decisions. I was serving at Mission 615 one Saturday and was out of the sound booth walking by the bleachers, and this guy said, "Hey, man, can you get me another sweet tea?" I said, "It may be out, but I'll go check for you." I went to the kitchen and filled up his glass and brought it back to him. He saw my kindness and servant heart and smiled. He thanked me and said, "I'm Gene." "I'm Wesley, nice to meet you," I responded as I shook his hand. Then he asked me for my phone number, and I thought he just wanted a friend so I gave it to him.

Gene called me one afternoon and didn't have anywhere to go, so I picked him up and brought him back to the student housing apartment. I wanted to help him out by letting him sleep on the couch, but eventually he overstepped his boundaries. One late night, he tried to make a move on me and touch me inappropriately while I was sleeping, and when I woke up, I was upset and freaked out. He knew he had done wrong and walked out, and I didn't hear from him for a while after that.

Another Saturday came around and I was finishing up the day at Mission 615, and my friend Kayla asked me if I could give her friend Thomas a ride afterward. I never met him so didn't know what he looked like, so after the last bus left and I turned off the computer and electronics, I started asking around for him. I eventually found him, a short guy, with dark hair and glasses. I greeted him and introduced myself. We were approaching my van, and he jokingly said, "I hope you don't mind riding with a gay Buddhist." I was respectful and said that's okay. We started talking, and I invited him to go out to eat at Buffalo Wild Wings with the leaders of Mission 615 and me. He accepted the offer. On the way there, I shared my testimony with him, and when we arrived, we went in the restaurant. My story touched his heart, and Cody led him in the prayer for salvation. Thomas accepted Christ as his Lord and Savior right there in the waiting line. Glory to God!

During dinner, the Holy Spirit was convicting Thomas, and he said, "I guess I need to do something about my homosexuality." Cody said, "Yeah, you're right." We finished eating, and Thomas didn't have anywhere to go because he was actually homeless. I didn't have the heart to put him on the streets, so I took him back to my student housing and let him sleep there for a little while. Hahaha! I wanted to save everyone back then.

Thomas and I got along great. I helped him out with food and shelter as long as I could, but eventually that would come back on me. One night, I was sitting at my laptop playing League of Legends and jamming to some metal, and my roommates and a couple of friends came in with a Ouija board. I knew what that was, and I sternly warned them, "Demons are real and you don't want to do that, I promise you." They were surprised, but because I didn't know them at all, they knew I wasn't joking around and they didn't open the Ouija board or use it. Satan was trying to get to me through whatever he could, so he sent this random girl from one of my classes to ask me if I wanted to be friends with benefits and I declined her.

One day I was out working and out of the blue, I got a call from Gene. He apologized for what happened, and I forgave him and allowed him to come back for a couple of days. Little did I know, my other two roommates across from me had a homeless friend that they were allowing to sleep on the couch in the living room. One night their friend came in late and tried to lay on the same couch as Gene, and he did not like that at all. Gene was upset and couldn't handle that, so he left again.

I tried hiding Thomas as long as I could, but the RA knew something was up. My roommates got found out and so did I. I was kicked out of student housing. Thankfully my roommate on my side had a friend moving into student housing and out of his apartment, and he offered to me to stay at his apartment for one month until his lease was up. So I thanked him and got the keys. I moved all my stuff into Tulip Grove apartments and had a peaceful stay for a month by myself. I love looking back and seeing how much God provided for me through different people when I was in need.

One day, Thomas decided to go to school with me at Art Institute and further his education. He filled out his FAFSA form and got accepted to receive Federal student aid, so then he started to attend Art Institute for himself and he was able to get into student housing and he had a place to stay.

The one month left of the lease of the apartment I was living at was about to be up, and I had nowhere to go again. I loaded up all my belongings and had to refuse most of the jobs I was called for due to having all my belongings in my van. Eventually after Thomas was in student housing, he allowed me to stay with him in Avalon apartments where he was living, and the RA saw my van there but didn't say anything thankfully. I stayed there for a couple of weeks, and that is how I met my friend John. John and I got along great and had a few different classes together at school.

John had schizophrenia and also had panic attacks. One night, he started having a panic attack and he had me take him to the hospital. I was driving fast and trying to get him there on time, but we ended up getting lost downtown and couldn't find the hospital. His truck broke down, and we were walking and following GPS on my phone. It ended up being the wrong address, and he collapsed and the ambulance came and picked him up from there. I asked someone to jump me off at his truck and it started, and I made it back to the apartments once I got it running. John was okay and recovered and was released the next day.

At the apartment one night, I was working on art and someone came over who went to school with us and his name was Eddy. We started talking about art and music and ended up becoming friends. I was on my computer one night, and this girl named Haley and her friend came over and were hanging out with the other roommates in the living room. I was playing League of Legends on my laptop, and we started talking and Haley came over and sat next to me. She was really cute, and I was interested in her so we started hanging out.

After two weeks at the Avalon apartments, I found a little duplex for rent nearby and I scheduled a showing. I went and met the owner and put in my application and got to sign my first lease with Tandem Realty and had a little duplex on Dodson Chapel road.

I was still keeping up that hectic schedule and going to school living by myself. I didn't have a bed of my own anymore, and my friend Stephen called me one day because he was getting a new mattress and offered me his old one. Galatians 6:7 says, "You reap what you sow," and the time I gave my mattress to David and Leah in Memphis was coming back around to me. It was a very nice king-size pillow-top mattress.

This was a blessing, but I was becoming complacent in my justifications for idolatry. Slowly but surely I was falling away from God despite all the good things happening.

CHAPTER 10

EDDY CHAPARRO

The duplex was a great spot for a couple months, but I was getting back into drinking again, playing too much video games, and downloading tons of secular metal music. I didn't have anyone around to stop me, and these were idols in my heart that little by little were dragging me away from God. I still would hang out with Haley while living there and would go over to her apartment and watching movies with her. Horror movies, dark and raunchy movies, and blasphemous shows like *Family Guy* and *Tosh.O*. These things grieved my spirit, but I was attracted to her and wanted to spend time with her. I made a move on her one night, and we started making out and things moved really quick. But the Holy Spirit empowered me to stop myself from going too far with her.

Work at Crosstown started slowing down around this time, and I was barely making ends meet. I got reconnected to Eddy who needed a place to stay. I didn't know it at the time, but he exploded and threw a TV through the window at the last apartment he was at and as kicked out. I didn't know Eddy well, but I took him in hoping that He would help me with my rent and finances. We got along great at first, but I soon found out there was something I didn't know about Eddy. He was bipolar and had explosive anger problems, and I was in for a wild ride.

I kept seeing Haley in this time and spending time with her. I would go see her, and she would come over to my place and spend the night. I was compromising with many things in my relationship with God and had purchased a Galaxy S5 and sought out and downloaded a lot of underground old-school death metal and death/doom metal from the '90s on my brand-new phone. I had accumulated some music and planned on listening to it later.

Next I purchased an iPod because of my music idolatry. I still loved Lauren all this time, but I lost her number when my phone was stolen while at work in the warehouse one day. I wanted to talk to her again, but I was patiently believing God would reconnect me to her when it was the right time but losing her number meant I had no choice and there was nothing I could do to find her again at that time.

One day while out driving doing jobs, Eddy gave me a call and said, "There's a guy named Charles here asking if when can give him a place to stay for a while." I didn't even hesitate and said, "Sure." I got home from work and met Charles for the first time. We became friends, and he helped encourage me and speak life to me when I was falling away. I didn't have much furniture, but God provided some free stuff to use temporarily and a nice sectional couch from my mom's friend for only $100. Charles slept on the couch, and Eddy and I each had a room.

Eddy and I would get along some days, but other days weren't so good. The smallest thing Eddy didn't like would make him explode with anger and we were at each other's throats sometimes, and Charles would be the voice of reason and peace. I took Eddy to Mission 615 to serve with me and he loved it. He was helping with inner city kids church and had a heart for the kids. He got a job at Electronic Express as a salesman, and I was hoping he would help out with bills. One weekend at Mission 615, Eddy and I met a guy named Ken. Ken was homeless and had lost everything due to his alcoholism and pride. He needed a ride after service let out, so we offered to give him a ride. After we talked for a little while, God spoke to me and Eddy to take Ken home with us and help him out.

I gave him $100, and we went and bought some beer because he wanted to. I helped Ken out for a while, and Ken told us powerful testimonies of evangelism and crusades he was a part of all over the world. He was great at witnessing to people and sharing Jesus with them, which is an area I wasn't very good at yet. God used Ken to teach me some things, and he was wise with spiritual things. He taught me to apologize makes you tenderhearted, to ask forgiveness makes you brave hearted, and to forgive all, enemies included, makes you Christ hearted. He told me a story of a crusade in Brazil that happened years ago where when he and the others went there. They were threatened by a witch doctor to not go through with it. They went through with the crusade anyway and thousands received Jesus, were healed, and miraculously touched by the Gospel of Jesus Christ and nothing happened to them. He found out years later a story of a man who was there the day of the crusade. This man was an assassin paid by the witch doctors to kill Ken and his team. The man got out his gun and started walking toward them, and an invisible hand slammed him to the ground and said to him in Portuguese, "*Touch not my servants and do them no harm.*" He got up and shook it off and starting walking toward them again, and the invisible hand slammed him to the ground even harder and said again even louder, "*Touch not my servants and do them no harm!*" The man didn't go through with it after that was actually saved and that was how he heard this story. Talk about protection while doing God's will. Despite telling me such powerful testimonies, Ken struggled with alcoholism and would drink my beer without asking and then hide the bottles in spontaneous places like inside the couch or under the bathroom sink. Especially because I kept craft beer around. Before long, I decided to take a break from school because I needed to catch up on bills and take all the work that I could. I was justifying my music and it started with "They only talk about politics, death, war, etc." and eventually progressed into "They only talk about torture and aren't Satanic or Antichristian." I got to the point where I had downloaded a few thousand gigs of metal and was pursuing that idol in my heart. I would justify and say, "They're only Antichristian in a poetic way and aren't hateful toward Christ." This went on and on until something had to be done. I was becoming very prideful, lustful, lazy, selfish, and was only thinking about myself. I was even missing Saturdays to go serve the homeless at Mission 615. I had Haley come over a few more times to hang out and even took her out on a couple routes with me to ride along, but when I started to get really far from God, her car broke down so she couldn't come over any more. My job and life were falling apart because I was committing adultery on my source and the sustainer of my life.

I made a trip back to a friend's place in Memphis to visit, and while there, I had a great time with him but didn't realize that there were demons there. That night, I fell into masturbation and looked at pornography because my spirit wasn't strong enough, and it felt like I was literally forced to do it. I hadn't sinned sexually like that in about a year and a half and knew I couldn't go back there any time soon.

Gene moved back in and there were six of us total, but Gene wasn't there for long because him and Ken didn't get along because they were both very prideful and butted heads. Eddy also didn't get along with Gene and was in his face threatening him and made Gene leave only after a couple of days. We were down to five of us now, and the financial troubles continued.

Eddy put holes in the walls, kicked the front door in and shifted the whole frame, and would lose all sense of judgment when he got angry. I tried my best to help him, but I was dealing with my own struggles at the same time.

Thomas was living with me for a little while as well because he stopped going to school and wasn't in student housing anymore. He turned away from God and got in a homosexual relationship with a witch and moved out. With another moving out, we were down to four of us.

Eddy got up one morning and got into an argument with me, and instead of letting me take him to work because I needed the van for work, he left in my van and took it to work a couple miles from the house. I was livid and I walked up to his job and used my extra key and took the van to get to work. Around this time, I had been spending four hours in worship every morning and most the time while I was driving, but as my love for extreme metal became stronger and stronger, I started spending less and less time with God. Even when I played worship music, my mind was elsewhere, and eventually I would cut my worship time short so I could listen to slamming brutal death metal instead.

I was working with Fabian at Crosstown because deliveries were getting less and less. One van repair after another until I had spent a few thousand dollars and things were getting rough for us. My van had broken down again, and this time, I had no way to get it back up and running again. My parents couldn't afford to help me out with it at that time, so I had no transportation.

My friend who I worked with named Fabian consistently picked me up for work with him doing deliveries through Crosstown while my van was broken down. This was enough to help me survive. Eddy only worked at Electronic Express for a few days, and when he got his first check, he bought monitor speakers and things to build a makeshift recording studio. He would stay up to around 2:00 and 3:00 a.m. blasting music, rapping, recording, etc., and we would be at each other's throats over that some days, yelling and not physical.

Ken helped me repair the door and the holes in the wall and taught me how to do those repairs with my own tools. Ken struggled with drinking and eventually left to go into the Hope Center and moved out. That made three of us remaining, Charles, Eddy, and me, and it remained us three for a good few months.

Eddy went with us on a youth trip to Gatlinburg called Accelerant. We heard a very powerful message from Sean McDowell about pornography and the science behind it. Eddy stood up among a few hundred others. It was exactly what Eddy needed to hear. Also during this conference, God was working on Eddy to forgive his parents, but he refused to.

After this conference, Eddy and I were much closer. He knew by my actions that I wasn't lying to him, and I truly loved him as my brother in Christ. I took Eddy on a trip with me and my family to

North Carolina, and while we were there, he admitted to me that he had contacted a woman through Craigslist and gone and slept with her. I forgave him and he broke down even more, and we became closer. Eddy started trying to control my life and would drive my van all the time, and I would let him because I didn't want to deal with his anger. Eddy would also speak the worst things to me, condemning me, calling me names, cussing me out, and calling me worthless and stupid. I put up with it because I didn't want to give up on him.

We were making it by because Charles was holding down his job at Mapco and would help me out with bills. My job with Fabian was keeping us afloat, but eventually, that slowed down as well. We were behind on rent a couple months and not sure what to do. This was only the beginning of the financial collapse in my life.

Eddy was my best friend some days and we would get along great and hang out, but the first wrong word and action from me and he would explode on me and make me want to die. Thankfully Charles would always lift me back up after Eddy tore me down. Eddy always told me what I needed to hear despite tearing me apart most days. Eddy, Charles, and I started seeking God and doing Bible studies together. Eddy set up for Charles and me to come eat dinner with his family, and when we came in, he called us his brothers.

The financial hardships were setting in, and I was finally broken down. Eddy and I were praying, and I repented. As I did, tears started flowing as the realization was setting in of all I had done, and Eddy knelt down with me with his arm over me because he knew my pain. I really tried after this to make things work out with Eddy, but his words were like a serrated knife to the soul on the days he would snap. Even after he used my van to go sleep with girls, I knew, and I forgave him again anyway. We would pursue God together, but Eddy just couldn't break free from his unforgiveness. One night, it was cold out and we went downtown and went around to look for homeless people who needed a warm place to stay for the night. We found two different guys who wanted to come with us. We made some fire ribs and gave them a meal and a place to stay for the night. We prayed over the meal, and it was amazing to do that for the homeless. It truly touched my heart. They both left the next morning.

The utilities were behind and about to get shut off, but we couldn't afford to stop it. So the electricity was shut off. We lived in the dark by candlelight and had to live off canned food. Thankfully, we still kept the water on during that time because I had to pawn my iPod and destroy one of my idols: music.

One day, police showed up at my place and asked for Eddy, and they arrested him. It turns out he stole studio equipment from Art Institute to pawn to try to help with rent. His dad and I bailed him out after a couple of days.

I hadn't heard from Thomas for a little while, and then one, day he called me and said, "You said being able to love others from the position of having been loved by God for yourself. I want that. I think I really need God in my life again." He broke up with the witch, and I let him move back in with us.

One day, Eddy took my van without asking at all, and I needed it that day. I called his dad and told him my situation that had been building up over time. I didn't know what else to do. Mr. Chaparro called Eddy and confronted him, and he was pissed at me. Thomas left to go walk and pray because the situation wasn't looking good. Eddy got home and came in screaming at me and spit in my face and pushed me down onto my bed. I stood strong because I wasn't going to fight him. His fight was with himself, not with me. He threatened me, and I said, "I don't want you to go to jail." This made him even angrier and rage was emanating from him. I tried to calm Eddy down, but it wasn't happening. Eddy took my phone and wouldn't give it back.

At this, I prayed in my heart for God to tell Thomas to call the police. I told Eddy he had to leave and that I couldn't take it anymore. He refused to listen or do anything I said. I stayed strong and waited until we had a knock on the door. It was two Metro Police officers. I explained the situation and told them he hadn't hit me or assaulted me because I didn't want him to go to jail. I didn't know spitting in someone's face was assault, so the officer thought I lied to him. The officer gave me the option of filing an order of protection to which I agreed. Once Eddy knew what happened, he fled and thought he was going to jail. I was given a ride down to the court house to file the order of protection.

Thomas came back after all that and said, "The Spirit of the Lord told me to call the police." I thanked him and told him what happened.

Things were finally stable for me because God was restoring my life again. My eyes were opened and there was no going back. My dad got a new car, and he gave me his Pontiac Vibe, which had three hundred thousand miles on it from him doing deliveries in it, but it was a great car nonetheless. They also helped me get my van back up and going. I was using my car and my van for deliveries depending on what size I needed. I was still behind on bills and had to get a loan from my friend Teddy to pay rent, and over time, I paid him back.

Thomas was there for a few weeks but eventually started trying prove to himself that he could keep homosexuality and God at the same time. He met someone online and they started talking on the phone for hours. Holy Spirit told me that he was trying to justify the homosexual lifestyle as not being a sin, but I didn't want to believe it. One day, Thomas says, "I need a ride to the bus stop so I can head to Detroit." I gave him a ride up there, and we said our goodbyes.

Only Charles and I remained, and we were trying to make ends meet but were way behind, and my job was not calling me as often. Eddy tried to reach out to me, but I couldn't communicate with him or he would get in trouble with the law. Mr. Chaparro called me and told me that he had to call the police on Eddy and that Eddy had fled and was on the run.

We told him we would be praying for them. One day, we were using my cargo van to load up Eddy's belongings and take them to his parents' house, and while doing that, Eddy starts walking down the street right by us. I didn't know what to do or say, and I definitely didn't want him to go to jail, so I didn't say anything.

Eddy tried to make amends with his parents after this. A couple weeks went by and I received a call from Mr. Chaparro. He said, "Eddy killed himself." I was so broken. I told Charles, and we embraced each other and wept.

Eddy's funeral was coming up, and Charles and I both went. I had the opportunity to stand up and speak at his funeral and tell of how Eddy brought me back to God and shared some of my testimony as Holy Spirit led me to speak. It was truly beautiful to see all the people that showed up for his funeral and remembered him well. I remember mourning him after that because he had such a beautiful heart and Holy Spirit spoke loud and clear to me: "He is at home with me now and finally at peace."

CHAPTER 11

OFF COURSE

It wasn't easy after Eddy had passed, but I managed the best that I could. The lease was about to be up, and Charles and I were behind again. I had to borrow money from Teddy one more time, but because I didn't pay him back in the time I agreed to last time, he wanted some collateral. So I told him to hold on to my laptop. This was all meant to happen because that idol needed to be crushed once and for all.

I paid rent and was only one month behind now. I opened my home to my friend Steven and his girlfriend in those last couple of months on the lease to help them out while they found a place of their own. I knew God was calling me to move north around White House, TN, so we all went and looked for a place. I followed Holy Spirit to the area I was supposed to move. We found a place owned by a sheriff who was moving. He had renovated everything. Two homes on the same property. I didn't take action on this, and by the time I asked my parents to cosign with me, we went up there to see the house. Shortly after, he already had another man come look at it and he jumped on it. This devastated me and I felt like a failure. Whatever God had for me there, I would be missing out on.

With the door I was supposed to walk through now closed, I had to figure out another option. Steven and Sarah left shortly after the opportunity to move to White House didn't work out, and they found their own place. Charles and I weren't sure what to do and the lease was up. Fabian helped us move some stuff to storage with his truck. Shortly after that, we moved in with Charles's parents for about four days. Then after four days, Charles's mom's friend Ms. Felicia opened her home to us to rent. We each had our own rooms for $400 per month. This was a much-needed season of rest for me. Charles got behind on rent due to not having a license or car and couldn't find a good job in walking distance. Ms. Felicia forgave him what he owed her and I stayed there. This was a steady and normal season for me. At one point, I decided to buy a thirty-two-inch Samsung TV and a PS4 with Diablo 3 and Elder Scrolls Skyrim. I played Diablo some in my free time and eventually bought a couple other games. One night, I decided to play Skyrim, so I started it up and played for one hour. The first mission was to burn incense and summon a spirit. The spirit said, "Clear out these grave robbers from my grave and I'll reward you." I finished the mission and then my desire to play just wasn't there at all. I stopped playing and started to read the Bible. I was directed to 1 Samuel 28 where Saul goes to the witch of Endor and she summons the spirit of Samuel. God cuts Saul off from being blessed after this because he did this abomination. I was like, "Okay, God, I get it." Next I sold the games for gas money and gave away my PS4 to my new home church Iris Nashville. I gave the TV away to an older woman named Pat whom Gene had met, and we helped her out to go to and from the grocery store some times. I tried to help Gene out but didn't know that his intentions at the time were all messed up.

Gene and I went to a revival night in Memphis one weekend, and the Holy Spirit fell so powerfully while we were there that I was weeping and being healed even more from being molested. I stood up and shared my testimony while I was there, and it touched so many hearts. A man who was there from the Hope Center in Memphis was planning on killing himself that night after the service, but God moved on his heart and he confessed that and gave the knife he was going to use to the leaders there and he accepted Christ. Gene was on the floor choking because of the demons that still wanted control, and he didn't let them leave.

God was healing me of my shame, fear, trauma, etc., and I could feel the difference. I still struggled with explosive anger problems though, and I didn't know what to do. I was having to spend most of my time everyday worshiping, praying, reading God's Word, etc., just to keep myself positive and sound minded.

I still would snap when something upset me and I didn't know why yet.

Toward September of 2015, Crosstown got a new contract with Vanderbilt doing home deliveries, and I started to do those routes. All of a sudden, Vanderbilt fell through on their contract, but it was right after Crosstown hired six new drivers. I wasn't getting enough work there anymore because of this, and the door was closing. This was the ending to my chapter with Crosstown Couriers.

I needed to find a new job, and I needed one very soon. I got a job through my dad with a company he worked for once before called Zip Express. I went in for my interview with the branch manager, Clarence. All went well. I finished my drug test and background check and was ready to go. I was given a start date, and then I had a problem. My cargo van wasn't running and was at Mr. Chaparro's house. I knew I was going to need it, so I prayed for God to make a way. I found a mobile mechanic named Chris. Chris and his younger brother came out to Mr. Chaparro's house and started working on my van. They figured out it was my differential that needed work, and the pinion had swelled up in the differential because I had driven it thousands of miles with no gear oil, and this wasn't going to be an easy fix.

We towed the van to a house Chris was renting to use as a shop, and the nightmare had just begun. Chris was able to use a Dremel tool to cut the horseshoe clip out piece by piece in seven hours and finally removed the swollen pinion. That was a good step, but it turns out the bearing and seals were ruined on both side. The brake pads needed to be replaced, the brake calipers were ruined, the differential needed to be replaced, and an axel on the passenger side needed to be replaced. We also needed a case of brake cleaning fluid to spray out the shards of bearings in the casing. This took about three days to finish, and every day, I had to tell Clarence what was going on and he was getting fed up with how long it took because their back up driver, Joe, was running the route I was supposed to take over. I hit my knees and prayed, "God, you know I need this job, and I ask that you give me favor to keep it." After we got all the parts and replaced everything but the axel, I took my van home to Ms. Felicia's house at 11:00 p.m., and I was ready to start work early the next morning.

I woke up with no sleep and rushed out the door, skipping my time with God and didn't read His Word. I got to the warehouse and sorted my route according to the training I had with Joe while we were working on my van. It was an *awful* day. I got lost, made mistakes, and lost my cool multiple times that day. It was so bad my other manager Mike gave me a map of Clarksville and told me to memorize it. I told them I would do better the next day.

The next day I spent time with God that morning before leaving, and it was a great day with no major problems and I remembered where to go this time. Toward the end of my route, I started hearing a shaking sound and feeling vibrating in my van. It turned out that the axel we thought we didn't need to replace was actually bowed and this completely destroyed the new bearings and seals on the passenger side. Chris was able to get the new parts that day, and we had some work to do *again*. It was terrible, haha. We got new bearings, seals, gear oil, and another case of brake cleaner to spray out the shards again. We had to break the brand-new seal we just replaced for the casing and drain the new gear oil full of metal shards. We sprayed out the entire casing *again*. I went to pick up the same axel we had just returned two days, and we finished all this in time for me to get to work that next morning. This was insane but we made it through, and I had a van completely rebuilt on the rear and ready for work now.

I worked at Zip Express just shy of a year and was told I needed to find another place to live because Ms. Felicia was selling her house and moving back home to Detroit. Right around that time, it was getting much colder outside, and one morning, I went outside to start my van and I heard a "*loud snap*," and my van wouldn't start.

I contacted my mobile mechanic and had him come take a look, and by the time we got it towed to his shop he was renting and had the top half of the engine disassembled, we found out that a piston had snapped in the engine and I had very little options of what to do as this is a very expensive and time-consuming repair. I went to U-Haul and rented a cargo van so I could stay afloat. I wasn't clearing much money, but it was a nice van and a huge blessing to me for a few weeks.

One day, a coworker and fellow Christ follower approached me and told me that Holy Spirit spoke to him to help me and allow me to rent one of his vans. He only wanted $600 per month, and compared to $80 per day, I accepted immediately. I drove this van a couple weeks and then decided to rent to own it from him. The price stayed the same, and he only charged me $3,000 for this 2000 Ford Econoline cargo van, and yeah, it was old and kind of rickety but I was so thankful and I gave God all the praise and glory for His faithfulness to me.

CHAPTER 12

DECEPTION PART 1

I was still talking to Gene at the time, and he needed a place to stay to get off the streets. I moved out of Felicia's and got a week stay hotel for one week with Gene expecting him to pay half. After that week passed, Gene couldn't hold up his end of the deal, so we both went homeless for a couple days. We found a cheap and weird place to live through Craigslist that was a commercial building converted into apartments owned by this very strange Chinese woman named Cindy.

We moved in and had one room that we shared that had just enough room for my king-size mattress and a small shelf. While here, Gene tried to make a move on me while I was sleeping, and I was pretty upset but I forgave him. I didn't know this yet, but Gene was dealing with a Jezebel spirit, the master manipulator spirit.

My dad got a new car and blessed me with his old one, a Pontiac Vibe with almost three hundred thousand miles, but it was free and it ran so I was thankful. I was driving in the Vibe one day, and I stopped at a stop sign near the apartment and didn't know that cross traffic didn't stop. I went to go and a pickup truck was barreling down the road, and I pulled out right in front of him, and when I noticed him right on me, I floored it and turned the wheel to the left as hard as I could. He slammed on his brakes and showered me with what was about ten ladders and scaffolding. I apologized and helped them pick up the ladders and scaffolding to put back up on his ladder rack and they said it was okay and drove off. Surprisingly, the sun roof wasn't busted out. I was amazed at God's protection over me that my car had very little damage, but the divine protection from heaven over His children's life doesn't run out but only continues because He is slow to anger and abundant in loving kindness for His children, even when we make mistakes.

I had used the Pontiac for my old job with Crosstown and put about thirty thousand miles on it. Now that I had two vehicles, and because Gene didn't have a car, I decided that I would sign it over to him. He used it for a while, and then it broke down in the parking lot where we were staying. I didn't have the money to fix it so it sat for a while.

Gene and I had planned on getting new cars so he could get a job and we could better help each other out. The Vibe had 330,000 miles and wasn't going to last much longer even if we had fixed it.

One day, Gene said that Holy Spirit spoke to him about taking out a loan, and because I didn't have enough discernment to know that he was using me yet and I was hoping to help Gene rebuild his life, I took a loan out through Advance Financial for $4,000, but we were only approved for $2,333. I gave him $2,000 toward a down payment to get a car. We went to get a car at a car lot, and he told me had gambled most of the money and had $500 left. They didn't want to accept a small down payment unless I cosigned for him. I thought that I was hearing God tell me to sign so I did, and I helped Gene get a Jeep Patriot at a terrible price with a high interest rate.

We left the car lot and went back to the janky apartment. Gene tried to get jobs but couldn't keep a job because of his struggles which had had him in bondage for years. I thought I was discipling Gene, but in reality, he was using me, which started to backfire shortly after.

He had only driven the car for a short time and someone ran a red light and T-boned him on the passenger side, and it was a miracle he survived with minor injuries. I went to visit him at the hospital and pray with him and encourage him. After he was discharged from the hospital, we went back to the same car lot to see what we could do next. We gave another $500 down payment and purchased a 2008 Mazda Tribute for us both to share this time. The first few months went by, and Gene could not stop gambling his SSI checks away and I kept making the payments because God was teaching me firsthand how to show *mercy* even when he didn't deserve it. He was teaching me this not for Gene, but for *me*, to cultivate Christ-like character in my own heart through my circumstances.

The last time Gene tried to make a move on me had me at attention, so I moved into my own room from then forward and he had his own room. I wasn't going to give up on him that easy though because so many people didn't give up on me when I committed horrible sins in my past against myself and others.

One day, I was asleep during the day and Gene tried again, and I was done at this point. I was furious with him and ready to get away from him for a while. Even despite his actions though, I didn't have the heart to let him go homeless again, so I forgave him and gave him another chance.

My uncle had just passed. I helped my aunt move out of her house, and she blessed me with many different kitchen utensils which I used to supply the kitchen where we were staying. We had a very nice Korean lady move in with us at the apartment, and she cooked for us and was a blessing to us.

We had a few more weeks in that place, and then Gene couldn't keep up with his payments so he was getting kicked out by the landlord. I didn't know what to do next, but when he asked my help, I couldn't say no.

CHAPTER 13

FORGIVENESS

At this time, I didn't have any place to keep my furniture, so I decided to give away everything I owned except for my bedding, clothes, and my CDs. I moved out with Gene and into another week stay hotel crawling with crime in a bad area, and it was here that God impressed upon me to forgive my molester and to send messages to those I had sinned against from my past.

You see, I thought I had already forgiven him because I prayed it out loud, "I choose to forgive ———." Though I hadn't truly forgiven him in my heart yet. I also needed to ask forgiveness from some other people. I sent the message and said simply, "I forgive you for everything you did to me. God bless you." He responded and denied it, but I felt a major shift within myself and my life. I didn't know it yet, but I was set free of my explosive anger problems that I had struggled with for thirteen years of my life. I had been day in and day out drowning my thoughts with worship music and prayer because I would explode in rage at the drop of a hat over small things and that was because the root cause of my pain, shame, depression, and anger had not been dealt with. I didn't know what to do, so I kept busy to keep myself from thinking about the pain and to numb myself from reality, but it only took two messages and then everything changed and I was set free!

I was beginning to hang out with my mobile mechanic and working for him some on the side. I made some money for a while, but eventually he stopped paying me. During that time, I met one of his oldest friends named Tim, and I shared my testimony with him and invited him to serve the homeless with me at Mission 615. It was there that he went forward for the altar call and received Christ. I was so proud of him, and it was amazing to see what God was doing in his life. He shortly after got baptized and fully involved with Mission 615 and was helping to reach the families and kids in the projects of Nashville.

I was at the week stay hotel for a very short amount of time before I couldn't afford it any longer because it was very expensive. I moved out and this time had nowhere to go, so Gene and I both were homeless living in our vehicles.

It was getting cold outside, and I was sleeping in my van in the parking lot at work and only one heating vent worked, so I had to put my blanket over that vent and cocoon myself under the blanket to stay warm. This was rough, so after a week, I started looking into Airbnb. I found a place ten minutes from the warehouse, so I contacted him and went to go check it out.

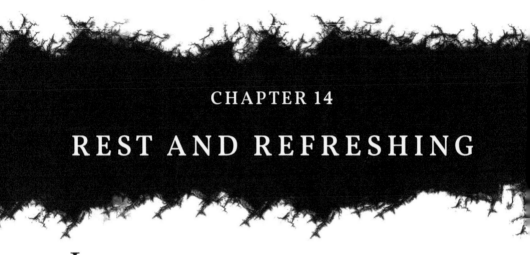

CHAPTER 14

REST AND REFRESHING

I followed my GPS to the Airbnb and went inside, and there I met Richard. The first thing I saw was a painting of Daniel in the lion's den and a book open on the table where Richard was learning Hebrew. I felt at home already. Richard was a retired navy vet and was full of wisdom and spent most of his time researching and studying. We hit it off immediately. I stayed with Richard for about a month, and then he upgraded me to the back bedroom with my own bathroom and shower. It was such a refreshing time after all the chaos and foolishness with Gene.

Richard and I studied deep biblical topics and watched YouTube together pretty often. We taught each other a lot of different useful information and watched many sermons together. I got to sleep in while living there so close to work and that was such a blessing in itself, and his company and a positive atmosphere made it even better.

After a few months, he got bed bugs and that was awful as I was getting tore up every night. We did some research and found a product online to spray to repel and kill them, so once we treated the apartment, they went away. That experience taught me to be grateful despite some annoying parasites tormenting me at night.

I hadn't heard from Gene for a while, and when he contacted me next, he had just lost his job. I called my friend Fabian to get him a job driving for him. One day when Gene was driving in Kentucky in Fabian's Ford Explorer, he went into a diabetic coma and blacked out behind the wheel at 70 mph and the car flipped multiple times and hit a tree. The car was on fire, and he broke his back from the accident. Though he didn't remember how he got out, it was definitely a miracle he survived.

He was in rehab for a while but recovered quickly. He asked me if Richard had a room he could rent, so I spoke with him and got him a room for $20 per night. That experience changed Gene for the better, but he still had the Jezebel spirit operating through him. I was making the payments on his Mazda Tribute, and I made one more before I didn't hear from him again for three days until he sent me a text saying he was going to Bethel in Redding, California, to go to school there because God told him to go there.

I enjoyed my time at Richard's place, and it was a time where I was growing much closer to God. With the extra time I had each morning being closer to work, I began spending forty minutes with God every day before work. Satan didn't like that and had a plan...

CHAPTER 15

BREAKTHROUGH!

My van was beginning to have engine problems, and I could not afford to fix it because of the Advance Financial loan payments they wanted from me with an extremely high interest rate. It was far more than I could afford, but I was stuck and couldn't get out of it. My debt was crushing me, and the vehicle problems on top of that didn't help.

I was on a visit to my parents one weekend, and I was lead in a prayer to receive my prayer language for the first time. I didn't understand how to at first and I only got one word, but once it started to flow, I kept repeating the same word and I had finally got it. It was storming severely outside, and there was torrential rain and strong winds breaking branches that were falling and hitting the roof and back deck. I went upstairs to sleep some until the storm had subsided before my drive back to Nashville. When I got upstairs, the Holy Spirit had me pray against the storm and I sung in the Spirit for the first time, and within minutes, the clouds split left and right and the rain and wind had completely stopped and all I could hear was the dripping of water off the branches from the trees. I was astonished! Then Holy Spirit said now go home, so I got my things and left. On the drive home, I practiced praying in the Spirit for three hours and felt totally different than I ever had.

When I got back to Nashville, I still had to figure out what I was going to do next, and so I surrendered my problems to God again. The good thing was my credit score was getting better, and I knew I needed a new van at this point. So I started looking around and found a lot in Dickson that had some great new Ford Transit vans available. I went out there and got the ball rolling and God backed me up with His favor. I found a Transit Van with twenty-three thousand miles and needed to find a loan with a low interest rate, so I started doing some research and found a place called Ascend Federal Credit Union. I set up an appointment with a loan officer and went in, and it went well! I was able to get a credit card with a $6,000 limit and pay off my Advance Financial loan with that and then pay the card back with a great interest rate! Praise God I got approved for the card and auto loan! I went from a 2000 cargo van to a 2016 Ford Transit van, and it was great! I was so thankful!

Now I was looking for a buyer for my 2006 van and for my 2000 van. I posted pictures online and started searching. A man messaged me and asked if I could take a lower price for them, and at first, I said that I needed more and kept looking, but after I didn't get anything else on them, I messaged him and asked if he was still interested and he was. He offered me a fair price for both of them, considering the 2006 needed a new engine and the 2000 was leaking oil. He drove up and picked them both up and took them off my hands, and the timing couldn't have been more perfect! Look at God's provision!

I was still on my Clarksville Route at work, and one day, I overslept through six alarms and multiple phone calls from my boss and I headed to work not knowing why I was so late until I arrived at my first stop. The moment I parked, a car parked at the *exact* same time as me. I unloaded the delivery and went inside and the girl who had parked knew the owner of the store. She was homeless and on drugs, living out of her car and struggling badly. The Holy Spirit had me share my testimony with her, and then it all made sense. God had set me up to be perfectly on time that day, not for my job but for a precious prodigal daughter who needed to experience the Father's love for her.

Very soon after that day, one of the other drivers was getting real sick with cancer and couldn't keep driving on his route, and so they offered me his route, which was much higher paying than my current route, so I accepted. I didn't realize how much driving I was going to have to do with this route, which was to Memphis, TN, and back to Nashville four days a week and Friday was only to Parsons, TN, and back. I also took a Saturday job unloading a truck and a Saturday route to Glasgow, TN. Things were definitely looking up for me, and I was working hard to pay off my debt in every way that I could.

CHAPTER 16

CLARKSVILLE

I hadn't heard from my friend Charles in a while, and he reached out to me. He had gotten a place to stay through Operation Stand Down and was having trouble financially and asked if I could move in with him to help me out, and he only wanted $100 per month, which would be huge savings for me and would greatly help him out as well so I accepted. I packed my things and moved in with Charles. The only problem was he had no air-conditioning, and it had started to heat up outside. I tried to stay with him, but it was too much to bear.

Gene messaged me and asked me if I could pay the payment on his car, and I told him no, I can't afford to. Then he said, "God told me to tell you to make the payment." My eyes were opened, and I realized he had been using me and taking advantage of my kindness, so I said that's it. I blocked him and cut ties with him.

I endured Charles's place for about two weeks, but even at night time in his apartment, it was ninety degrees or higher and I could barely sleep. My route to Memphis including my commute was six hundred miles per day four days a week, plus all the other extra work I was doing on top of that, which came out to ten thousand miles per month of driving.

One day I was driving home from Memphis, and I was barely staying awake. I had a close call where I had fallen asleep briefly and was immediately supernaturally woken up before I rear-ended someone in front of me on the interstate. I knew I had no choice but to move out and find another option.

My friend Tim had reached out to me and said that he had moved to Clarksville and was staying with his girlfriend Raven and that they wanted to rent the room at her apartment out for $250 per month, which was a fair price, and then I would have amenities and be able to sleep well. I didn't pray about this decision, but I was always looking for ways to lead people to Jesus and I knew that Tim needed my help in his walk as a new believer.

I moved in with them, and it was fine at first but quickly went south. Tim was struggling with drugs, and he was also sleeping around behind Raven's back. This was not a good environment, but I tried to endure for a while.

They were constantly fighting and at each other's throats, and I came home to the most toxic environment I had ever experienced. I would walk in and the most godless filth would be on the TV, and it tormented me. Plus the atmosphere was just horrible—anger, rage, deceit, etc. I often would put my headphones in and just retreat to my room to pray and worship because I could not take it.

Then they started physically fighting and the tensions would escalate further, and I didn't know what to do about it. I kept to myself but it was difficult. I was thinking I was making the right decisions but didn't realize what was happening. We were struggling hardcore, and I just thought it was things going wrong at the time. I gave Tim $500 for bills and then he told me his wallet got stolen. I was stressed but I didn't think anything of it. God provided it right back. Tim and Raven would fight often, but one of the times police got called was on Tim and he was arrested. The bail bonds in the area helped him out greatly. I had been using my credit card to try to help everyone, and I withdrew $800 to help Tim pay off his court costs from when he was arrested.

I was on my way to Memphis one day, and it was raining very hard and I felt like I was heavy enough in my van that it was handling well enough. I was driving too fast, and I went to pass someone in the fast lane and switched lanes into standing water and immediately turned sideways to the left and flew off the road. I was trying to get the van to turn back to the right as I was barreling through the muddy grass and had barely any control, and I was flying toward the cables on the oncoming side. I cried out to Jesus as I thought I was going to die, and then I slammed into the cables with the front driver side corner of my van right at the exact moment as a semitruck was passing and those cables were damaged, but I know God stopped me from going further than the cables or getting crushed by the semi. I was shaken up and pulled back onto the fast lane and kept driving, and I took the next exit to survey the damage. I had no mirror or headlight on the driver side, and the van was scratched along the side but still able to be driven. I filed a claim with my insurance company and scheduled a rental van with Enterprise for that same day. I drove the rest of my route and made it back to Nashville to pick up my rental van and drop off my van at the body shop.

I heard back from the body shop a few days later, and the damage was all cosmetic and structure damage but was enough for the van to be considered totaled by my insurance company. This was a long process while I waited to get my power of attorney form in the mail. The rental was covered up to a certain point, but that date was fast approaching. It turned out that the POA form was lost in the mail, and I couldn't afford to pay for the rental myself. The days were adding up, and before I knew it, I owed over $1,000 for my rental. I prayed and surrendered this to God and my dad called the insurance company and told them it wasn't my fault the POA form was lost in the mail and they agreed! I only owed for two days, which was $180! The POA form finally came in and I went back to the lot in Dickson for another van, and my insurance was able to cover most of it. I got my loan transferred over to my new van!

I closed out my claim and upgraded my insurance and purchased new vehicle coverage and everything I needed just in case. Well, I ended up needing it sooner than I thought.

I was out driving that Saturday and had finished my route and was on my way back from Glasgow, KY, to Clarksville via a road from Russellville, KY, on a single lane road, and suddenly a car comes *flying* around the oncoming lane passing three cars and crashing into me head on!

I had a wooden plaque in my windshield at the time that said, "Be still, and know that I am God."

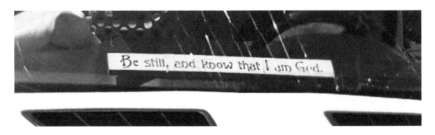

It happened so fast I couldn't even react or hit the brakes, and I was conscious through it all. The airbag had deployed and hit me in the face faster than I could see. Two cars back was an ambulance, so right when it happened, he pulled up and started checking me out. I was in the back of the ambulance, and I called my parents to tell them what happened. I found out the woman that hit me didn't make it and had died on impact. I was amazed at what just happened. I wished I could have done something to prevent it, but there was nothing I could have done. They took me to the hospital and started checking out my injuries. Police came in and took a blood sample to test in case I had anything in my system. I had been sober for a while now and had nothing to worry about. I was in the X-ray machine and the Holy Spirit spoke to me that I was going to be on *700 Club*. The X-ray revealed that I had a tangerine-sized hematoma of internal bleeding that was caused by the seat belt, and because of this, I was transferred to Vanderbilt and they took me into the ER and it felt like a TV show. I had fifteen different people attending to me at the same time, and when they were done, I was taken up to the ER floor. I didn't know this yet, but pictures were already posted online and many people knew what happened and were praying for me. I was given some pain killers and told they would check my vitals again in the morning.

The next morning, I awoke and they took my vitals, and the hematoma was *completely healed*! All glory to Yahweh! My God and my *Healer*!

I found out afterward that had I not been there, the ninety-three-year-old woman behind me would have been hit instead of me. Her life was saved because of God's timing. I also found out the ambulance driver behind me said, "Had I not filled out my paperwork for five minutes, then I would have been the one hit." Wow. So many miracles about this near-death experience.

I was discharged from Vanderbilt after only one night and was taken back to my parents where I could rest and recover. I contacted my old friend's stepdad to see if he would take my case, and he agreed to it. I was out of work over two months healing. Once I had made enough of a recovery to get back to work, I moved back to Clarksville. I closed out my settlement and made $18,000. I paid off some debt, bought a new HP Omen laptop, a computer desk, chair, Razer Mouse, wrist rest, and also launched my clothing line The World Hates Me. I printed my first batch of shirts and bought business cards. I kept $1,000 in my van in case I needed it.

After I returned to Clarksville, it was back to the same toxic environment. I bought Tim a new prepaid phone so we could communicate, but because he had been cheating on Raven, she grabbed the phone and threw it out the car window. Tim had gotten in a fight with Raven, and the police were called and she was arrested. We bailed her out, and quickly after that, they were in a fight *again.* This time when she got arrested, she came back and the apartment gave us a three-day notice that we were being evicted. I didn't have the heart to allow them to go on the streets, and Raven had many pets as well. I prayed and asked God to open a door for us, and we started driving around and looking for a place to go. We found one potential place, but it was a run-down trailer park and I wasn't going to do that.

The third day arrived and we had nowhere to go yet, and I found a nicer trailer park that had been converted into mobiles homes with hardwood decks outside each house. We went into the office and put in an application and despite my credit and our backgrounds, the manager said, "I'll give you a place to stay." The favor of God yet again! We moved in and the nightmare began…

CHAPTER 17

DECEPTION PART 2

We all three loaded up our things and all the pets and their cages and moved in the next day. By this time, I was talking to the company that the Mazda Tribute was cosigned through for Gene. We had been tracking the GPS tracker on it and monitoring it. It was in California for a while but eventually started heading back east.

The first couple of weeks in the new place were calm, and we didn't have any issues but that would change soon...

The fights started back and I couldn't take it. I was livid. I spontaneously took Tim to Illinois one night and dropped him off so he could take a break from being around Raven. She exploded when she found out because she had been trying to control him, but he had been using her, using her car and racking up debt with her cards. I didn't know all this until now. Now I don't know what to do. I cut communication off with Tim for a while, but he called me from his friend's profile one day and I answered and agreed to come pick him up. I had given him my tablet to use for communication while there, and by the time I picked him up, it was gone. He said he had been arrested and it was confiscated and I believed him.

The Mazda Tribute had come all the way back from California to Illinois and was picked up by a tow truck and brought back to Nashville. I went and picked it up and took the payments over. I brought the car back and was allowing Raven to use it for work because her car was repossessed because of Tim. Raven wasn't helping me with bills despite me allowing her to use the car. One morning I woke up to them screaming at each other and fighting, and I punched a hole in the wall by reaction and then came out and tried to break it up. It was too much and Raven was done at this point, and she arranged for a friend to come and pick her up and take her to North Carolina. Tim and I gave all the animals that were left away to good homes because we weren't going to be able to take care of them.

It was a much calmer atmosphere once she was gone. Right after that, I just knew to check inside Tim's bag in the bathroom and I found a handful of unused needles and my heart dropped because I knew he was using heroin. I confronted him on it, and he tried to lie and hide his intentions. He stole $100 from my van, and that time, he confessed after and I forgave him. I didn't want to give up on him, so I did everything I could for him to help him rebuild his life and get clean. We would pray together and watch sermons together but more was going on than what appeared to be.

Raven contacted me and I felt sorry for her and was willing to give her another chance, so Tim and I went and drove to North Carolina and picked her up to bring her back on the agreement that she would help with bills. God opened a door for her to get a job at a pet store and get her old job back. The same thing happened with the fighting between Tim and her after only a couple months and she still wasn't helping me with bills, so I told her she had to leave. She started working on leaving again, but it wasn't going to be quick or easy. It was a difficult time leading up to her second time leaving, but it came before we knew it. Her mother was moving back to North Carolina, and it worked out that she could ride back with her.

After she left, I asked my friend Richard to help me drive the car back from her dad's place where she left it, but she left the car with the gas light on. Despite that, we were able to get the car back to the house thankfully. After Raven left, Tim came back for a short while, and God lead me to search his bag in my bathroom and I found a massive handful of brand-new needles. I already knew what to do, so I took and threw them all away. Unfortunately, he found them later and got them back out after I confronted him. I tried to give him one more chance to get his life right.

I invited Charles to come move in with us to return the favor he had shown to me, and he took me up on that offer. He was a great roommate and brought some much-needed peace and wisdom. We studied the Bible together and worked out often. We were struggling financially, and one weekend of his serving in the army reserves, he brought home enough food to feed an army (pun intended). He brought back fifteen angus patties, fifty apples, fifty oranges, four pounds of cheese, and so much more! God used that to provide for us for a couple weeks! His provision and timing are always perfect.

I allowed Tim to use the car for work, and he got a construction job. I bought him $260 worth of tools for concrete work, and immediately after, he took a trip with someone to a funeral of someone he knew and said he sold all the tools for gas money. He worked at the job for a couple months, but I never saw any of that money. I didn't realize how bad off on heroine he was, but I wanted to help him. Eventually he started asking me for money saying it was for suboxone or subutex, basically drugs to withdraw off heroine. I helped him a few times with that thinking I was helping him withdraw and get clean. It was such a sad situation because I truly believed I was helping him to get his life right, and he was leading me on the whole time despite my efforts, and that is what hurt the most.

Next thing I knew he was telling me that someone broke into the car and stole my $300 tool set that I had just bought. Then Charles's knives that he bought in Alaska went missing. Things started coming to light quickly, but I never expected what was about to happen next.

I was at Kroger getting groceries, and this woman approached me and asked me for some money. I helped her, and then afterward, I got to pray for her and it was awesome to see God moving on her as tears were streaming down her face from the love of God all over her. This was a beautiful moment, and I believed God wanted me to help her so I got her number. I helped her a few times with vehicle repairs by withdrawing from my Advance Financial account again, one repair after another, and eventually she's saying that her mom is dying in the hospital and she needs money again. Long story short, despite the beautiful moment of God working on her and her spiritual needs being met, she was still an addict and she conned me out of $750.

My Memphis route was wearing me out around this time and I had a few close calls with getting sleepy behind the wheel, and so I prayed and asked God to deliver me from this. It wasn't long after that that one day I pulled up to the warehouse door in Memphis as usual and I waited. Two hours had passed and that wasn't normal. I usually had to wait but not that long, so I knocked and there was no answer. I called my boss and told him and he said he would call me back. Ten minutes later, he called and said that the place had gone out of business and to head back. The route had fallen apart and my income was drastically reduced from $320 per day to $125 per day, and then I really had to trust God. I worked that small route for a couple weeks, and eventually they cut another route in half and gave me more stops. This worked out for a couple months but still wasn't enough to cover my bills and expenses.

One week during the snowy winter, I was on my way east toward my first stop in Parsons, TN, and I had *no* tread left on all four of my tires, so bad that I almost slid off the road multiple times on my way down there. So after I did my delivery, I found a tire shop right down the street and bought four new tires using my rent money because I had no choice. The next half of my route was on curvy hills with no guard rails, and I couldn't take that chance. I had no rent money now, but I prayed and trusted God, and the day of my rent being due, I got a call from my parents saying that God spoke to them to help me with anything I needed. My rent was priority, so they helped me out and I was so thankful!

The car that I had allowed Tim to use eventually broke down and was left in a parking lot. I worked so much and didn't have time to get it towed back. I was blessed with a new route at work to swap with mine, and this one was to Glasgow, KY, and paid $180 per day and was much better. I loved this route. I finished around 11:00 or 12:00 p.m. every day and the people were so friendly. Over time, I was able to pay off my Advance Financial loan and get back to a zero balance. Every time something would arise. God would provide a way out as He always did. but some things were about to come to light and I wasn't ready for what happened next.

I was offered a new job as operations manager for third shift, and because of being salary and no extra gas expenses, I agreed to it. I began training and had to be there at 4:00 a.m. for a few days. Tim had brought someone over named Chad, and I only met him briefly and didn't think anything of it.

My week to start training, I went to sleep at around 10:00 p.m. and was woken up by a phone call at twelve thirty by Tim who was being arrested. He told me that the van was on the side of the road and where it would be, so I woke right up and started thinking of who to call. So I called my landlord George and told him what was going on. As I'm on the phone and walking up the hill at the park where I live, I'm approached by a police officer, and he said, "You look troubled. What's going on?" I told him that my roommate was arrested and my van was on the side of the road and that my landlord was on his way to pick me up and take me to get my van. He then asked, "Who is your roommate?" I responded, "Tim." He then asked, "Is there someone named Chad staying with you?" I told him yes, for two days, and I had never met him before. Turns out, there were three police cars parked at the side and they asked if they could come down there with me. I responded, "Yes, I have nothing to hide." They followed me down the hill and we walked inside, and because Chad had a warrant for his arrest, they put him in handcuffs and started questioning him about some stolen guns and then they asked me if they had permission to search, and I told them "Yes." They pulled back the couch and pulled out some *very* nice high-tech black rifles and some pistols that Chad and Tim had stolen. I was shocked and had no idea what was going on. They confiscated the guns and took Chad to jail. My landlord arrived to pick me up and took me to my van. When I arrived, there was someone who was with Tim there at my van, and I offered him a ride, but he said, no, someone was on his way to pick him up. I left and was able to make it to work on time to start training. What a crazy night!

Two weeks went by and it was just me and Charles. No drama, lies, or deception, and it was great. One night, Tim showed up at the door, and I told him he had to leave and that he couldn't come back so he left. A couple other weeks went by and then he shows up again being dropped off by some brand-new 2018 Mustang. I told him the same thing, and he said he just came to get his stuff. He came inside and started guilt tripping me the whole night, and I stayed up all night because I couldn't trust him. It was pretty awful, just being guilt tripped for hours after all I had done for him. When the sun came up, my friend Mark and his wife were coming over to use our laundry machines as they had planned, and when they arrived, I asked them if I could move in with them and I would help them with rent and they agreed.

I started packing up my stuff and Tim was calm at first and playing innocent, but before long, he started exploding and stumbling over his lies. It turned out he also had a Jezebel spirit and it manifested, and he started verbally attacking me and Mark while I loaded my van with my belongings. I wasn't going to take it anymore, so after I loaded my things, I was out of there.

I moved in with Mark and his family, and that lasted a couple months. The whole time I was praying about Tim being at my house that was in my name. Living with Mark's family was a fun time and a blessing after all that chaos and toxicity. The challenge of staying there was that I slept during the day and was working third shift at night for my new job, and they had two pet pigs, Pumba and Dudley, who didn't care that I was trying to sleep, haha. They gave me ear plugs, and I made due with that but those pigs were loud and you could hear their hooves clacking on the wood floor loudly and they would grunt and make so many different noises. Dudley was cool, but Pumba didn't like me. It was so weird. He unplugged my mini fridge and pushed it back to the wall so we couldn't tell and all my fresh berries went bad. Pumba even bit me three times just out of nowhere. Despite my swine dilemma, I enjoyed everyone's company.

It took me a while to open back up and let my walls down after being used and betrayed so many times, but God was restoring me back to a humble servant.

Mark's family had so many problems arising due to one bad circumstance after another, and they needed help with rent. So I prayed for three days about taking out the money from my Advance Financial loan, and I felt like God would back me up. So I went ahead and withdrew $700 and took care of it.

During this time, Tim was living in my old place and I told him because I have to pay the rent anyway to just give me the money for utilities and he could stay there until the lease was up. I never got anything from him though, and so the utilities were shut off and he *still* lived there and brought a single mom in there with a child. I had to keep checking with George about what was going on there, and thankfully the leasing office was directly across from the house and had cameras. That protected me, but eventually it started getting bad despite Charles living there and he had to leave as well, which was understandable. Once Tim had that girl and a child in there with no utilities, I started getting eviction threats and they would have been in my name. I really started praying harder then because I didn't want my credit to get any worse than it already was. Charles's mom told me the same thing that Holy Spirit was saying to get my name off that lease now.

Turns out that the girl and her child had moved out, but Tim was still there and he had allowed this girl to move in who had multiple warrants and was a drug dealer. I had no idea about any of this until later on. The girl had stolen from Tim, and so he threatened to call the police. She had fled but not before she and someone else tried to come steal the Mazda Tribute that was broken down outside. They were unsuccessful thankfully, and God had moved on my behalf and intervened again! His mercy is so hard to even comprehend, and He is so willing to fight our battles. Tim still had not left yet, and so I kept praying. Finally at the last minute, he moved out!

I still had to figure out what to do with that Mazda that I couldn't afford now, so I called the dealership and told them it's not running and the guy who cosigned wasn't making any payments. I was able to get the car towed back to the shop at the dealership for repairs. After though, I told them to keep it because there was no way to pay for it.

The most intense and difficult time of my life was in Clarksville, TN, and it was just about to come to an end. *Thank God!* Many lessons were learned about discernment and how to hear the voice of God. Most importantly, I learned that you can't save everyone, and that if someone is unwilling to change or listen, you have to keep moving and find those who *are* willing to change and listen to the truth.

I was working at the warehouse one day and a good friend and fellow believer told me if I ever need a place to go that I could stay with him. I waited a bit longer as I wanted to help Mark and his family a bit longer, but that one-hour drive to and from work and church every week was too much, and I needed a change. So I took my friend up on his offer and moved back closer to Nashville once again.

CHAPTER 18

SERVANT LEADER

I stayed with my friend for two months in Hendersonville, and it was only fifteen minutes from the warehouse. As I learned to be an operations manager, it was a great lesson in practicing obedience to the Holy Spirit and also making sure everything was neat, organized, and the flow of everything was going well. Not to mention 70 percent of my time there was alone, and I kept that place filled with worship music and I worshiped God every night when I got to work. I liked practicing organization as I wasn't the most organized before getting a job like that.

I was the type to help anyone sort their route, load their van, etc., as long as it helped the flow of things. I also learned to obey Holy Spirit in the smallest things the whole time. Another thing I loved about this time was learning what shepherding was all about. Looking after each driver and helping whenever problems arose. This was a different type of lesson for me, and it was crucial in refining my character into who I would need to be for my future.

It was a pretty easy job until we got a new contract, which was auto parts. I thought I would be getting a raise because of how much more work it was, but that didn't happen. I was told to come in an hour earlier and see if I had time that way. Those auto parts made that job a pain, and I would come in some night and see five or six eight-foot-long and ten-foot-high pallets of auto parts and even tires that I had to sort and scan. It was not easy, but we never know why things happen until after the lesson is learned.

They hired a few drivers to deliver the auto parts, and I became friends with them. I got to know them and the others there in the night and plant seeds in their life. One particular guy had never known God but knew of him, and one night, I was able to share my testimony with him. Maybe the account happened solely for him or maybe it was also for my own character. I learned that even alone, I had to stop complaining because it was changing my perspective. Proverbs 18:21 says, "The power of *life* and *death* are in the tongue and those who indulge in it will eat its fruit."

Instead of coming in and complaining about how much harder my job was or the fact that my pay stayed the same, I just worshiped instead. I kept my focus on God and not on what was in front of me. This changed everything! I didn't even care about my situation any more. I was too focused on seeking God.

When problems would arise, my managers would ask me to drive the company van and go out on deliveries after my shift which as long as I was paid more I was fine with that. One day, one of the drivers couldn't make it in, and they wanted me to run the route. I shouldn't have pushed myself that much, but we live and learn. I loaded up and ran the route, and when I was half a mile from the last stop where I could have delivered and then taken a nap, I fell asleep behind the wheel.

I woke up and had side swiped a car that was passing me because it was a single-lane road. Thankfully no one was hurt and God protected me and the other driver. I was honest, and I told them I had already been up all night working, and then I was sent out on that route. I had fallen asleep directly next to him as he passed me. The timing couldn't have been better. My manager drove and picked me up after all the info was traded between the other driver and me. This event would keep me from being allowed to drive for the company any longer and that was probably a good thing because I worked myself too hard sometimes.

I was living in Hermitage, TN, at this time, and things were great at home living with my good friends. One day, I met someone online, and she messaged me and we started talking. We exchanged numbers and started talking on the phone and we talked for hours on end. I thought that God had sent her into my life because she talked the talk and seemed to want to help people. She would say all the right things and flirt with me, and so I pursued for a short time. She drove from NY down to meet me, and I wasn't in any rush for a relationship. But I wanted to help her get to a good place. This didn't last long because some things were not right. We would do deliverance sessions with people on the phone and online, and it seemed like she was operating through the Holy Spirit. I told friends about her and thought she was going to be my wife, but darkness was about to come to light quickly because many were praying for me.

We caught her in her lies, and before anything else could happen, she fell for ex again and decided to leave and go get back together with him. I was deceived and thought things were going to move forward. And so afterward, I was heartbroken, but that Sunday, the sermon was titled "Hope as Warfare." It was *exactly* what I needed to hear. One verse stuck out to me, and it was Proverbs 13:12: Hope deferred makes the heart sick, but when longing is fulfilled, it is a tree of life.

Deferred means to choose or delay, and I was choosing to not hope and it made my heart very sick. I didn't understand what was happening, but after she had left, things began to come to light. She was a witch and had actually been sent by Satan to destroy me. She didn't operate through the Holy Spirit even though it appeared that way. She was a psychic, and even though she had power, it was actually demonic power. After that sermon, I decided that I was not going to choose to delay my hope but instead to worship God and not be moved by my own understanding and human frailty, so that's what I did and everything changed from that point on.

I was learning about how to live a generous life and live like Jesus did, and I would tithe my 10 percent as usual. I also would set aside $100 to give to any person that Holy Spirit told me to. I was in the car with my roommate and saw a homeless couple in the median, and I knew in my spirit that they were the ones to give it to. I asked him to pull over so I could. I approached them, and when I gave it to them, I also got to pray with them and it was amazing!

The way God blessed me after that was far more than I expected. I would drive my cargo van to work, and on days when others had vehicle problems, I would rent it out to them and one of the drivers needed it that week and rented it from me for six days and I made $500. I was blown away. Speechless. When Holy Spirit says to give and we obey, He has no limits as to how He can reward us, and sometimes it's not with money, but rather with time, rest, friendships, and other things we enjoy and He knows are good for us.

I worked that job for about a year, and it was wreaking havoc on my health. I started praying about what to do next. I felt like I was supposed to go into full-time ministry, but my finances were stopping me from doing that.

One morning while I was unloading a truck at the warehouse, the driver was running late and everyone was waiting on him to arrive so they could load up what they needed for their route. I was unloading the final pallet, and before I got in the truck, he was in such a rush that he misheard me and thought I was done and he flew off the dock with me in the back of the truck and adrenaline kicked in as he was flooring it. So I went back into the nose of the trailer and slammed the electric pallet jack into the wall next to cab multiple times to get his attention, which eventually worked. He stopped the truck and came around to the back, and I ran down and was upset but forgave him. I got in the truck with him, and the Holy Spirit took over the conversation and I was able lead him in a prayer to break generational curses that he had been dealing with his whole life. We got back to the warehouse, and he was saying that he was running late for Sabbath, which is why he was rushing so much, that irony…

It was fun though and I didn't die, so that was good. My manager joked that I shouldn't have left work while on the clock without asking. All the other drivers got a kick out of it as well. You never know how God will use you and give you some excitement in your Christian walk.

Since the incident with me driving, they couldn't send me out alone, but they could send me out with other drivers to help them run the route and show them where to go which I agreed to. I did this a good few times, but there was more to this than I thought. One day I had to go out with a coworker, and I had known that she was a fellow believer, but what I didn't know was that our stories were very similar and she had also been molested. We had a heart-to-heart talk, and I got to pray for her for healing in her mind and for the trauma to be removed from her memory. How beautiful is the Father's heart for others that He would use my mistakes and my suffering to set me up to bring healing to others. Incredible.

After this took place, the job was about to end because God was done using me in the place where I was and I had finally stopped complaining and keeping myself from moving forward. I may have understood that concept but finally applying it not only changed my mood and perspective everyday but eventually changed my circumstances. It says in God's Word that the Israelites were delivered by Moses's leading out of slavery in Egypt and then wandered the desert for forty years on what would have been an *eleven-day* journey. The Bible says that they "murmured and complained." The word for *murmured* in Hebrew actually means to "dwell," and they had chosen to dwell in a place of complaining and unbelief, refusing to have faith or believe God for what He had prepared for them. I didn't want to be stuck in a situation that I was overworked and underpaid any longer, and so I became intentional about keeping my words and thoughts from complaining. That's when God started really moving.

I was contacted by my friend who I only knew online, and he said, "I'm driving from Portland Oregon and going to Orlando where Holy Spirit is calling me to go and would like to meet you." I said, "Yeah! Come on by and we'll meet!" We met at a coffee shop and got to talking and I told him that I was behind on my rent some, and he offered to pay it and so I accepted. He was a Lyft driver, and it turned out that Nashville was one of the best markets in the country. He worked a couple days and helped me pay my rent. After that, he was told to help get me out of my job, so we started looking into our options. Lyft had a program where you could rent a car through Hertz and pay for it weekly by your rides. I applied and was accepted! I was making $150 to $200 or more per day on the weekends, and so I put my two weeks' notice in at the warehouse. They brought in a replacement, and I trained him for a week or so during my final two weeks. And then the day he was supposed to start, he didn't show up. I had no idea until I got a call later but that door was closed and that was out of my control anyway. I was able to rent my van out to a driver there at the warehouse and let him take over the payments, and it was a win-win situation. With my van taken care of and a new opportunity before me, it was time to go into full-time ministry, except it was not what I was expecting.

CHAPTER 19

LYFTED UP

I was given a ride to Hertz to choose my rental car and get my amp and start driving for Lyft, and I was able to get into a 2018 Chevy Malibu! It was such a nice car and so much fun to drive as well! This was going to be awesome! I started driving that night and took Josh's advice to start at around 6:00 or 8:00 p.m. and then drive for fourteen hours. I was making money so fast and was able to eat healthy as I wanted to and pay off some debts. It was truly a blessing. I tried to get my own car so I could make more money, but Josh and I didn't get approved. This was the best practice of obeying the Holy Spirit that I had ever had. Every day, He would tell me turn by turn and light by light and would map my day out. I kept worship music playing most of the time and just worshiped God in between rides. I was able to share my testimony with hundreds of people, and I even got to lead four people to pray the Sinner's Prayer and receive the Holy Spirit!

I was in Hermitage washing the car and detailing it, and then I finished and Holy Spirit said to turn the app on. So I did and I immediately got a request less than two miles away, and when I pulled up, a woman came running out with her daughter in her arms. She said she needed a ride to the ER because her daughter had a fever. I quickly drove them there, and when we arrived, I got to pray for them before they left. I had so many rides where people would share their whole life story with me and then ask me to pray for them. I was honored to be used in so many different people's lives. I got to share the truth of God's Word with people of all walks of life and all while making the most money I ever had, which provided for all my needs and then some.

One night, I was driving and got a request at a restaurant, and when I pulled up, there was an ambulance outside. So I prayed for them as I always do for emergency vehicles, and then the rider came out and told me his brother was in the ambulance and had just passed out and that I was supposed to follow the ambulance to the hospital. I had to drive pretty fast to keep up, and when we arrived, I got to pray with them for his brother and for them. No one can tell me that the Christian life is not exciting. If we just obey His voice, amazing things can happen.

I kept my car full of the presence of God and got to share wisdom and ultimately peace with so many people. It was truly an amazing time in my life. I talked to people who were lost in sin, struggling with homosexuality, transgender, drinking to numb their problems, and people who just needed some encouragement that day. I honestly don't even know all the lives I was used by God to touch as a Lyft driver and I may never know, but God honors our obedience.

Josh was on a trip to Phoenix, Arizona, to drive Lyft where there was a great market for ride sharing and he wrecked his car, but it was still drivable. So we prayed about what body shop to take it to, and the one we were led to was in Arkansas. We took a trip, and I followed him and we put the car in the shop. After returning to Nashville, we started renting with HyreCar, which is basically an app to rent a commercially insured vehicle from an individual and pay for it through the app, similar to Airbnb but with vehicles. We found a car in Boston, Massachusetts, that was very affordable and nice for Josh to use long term while his car was in the shop, so we took another trip. We headed up to Boston, and when we arrived, I tried to transfer my region over through Lyft and they wouldn't do it. When Josh tried to transfer to use the rental car in Massachusetts, there was an additional background check, which pulled something up on his record that deactivated him for good. We were stranded, so what we did next was went to my bandmate's house in Connecticut to work on my Christian death metal project Gog and Magog and take some preorders to get the gas money we needed to get back to Nashville. We were there about three weeks and recorded some new songs and revised and cleaned up old ones that needed to be re-recorded, and we started doing promotions and making teaser tracks. We took enough preorders after we finished recording the album and left back toward Nashville.

On our way back, we stopped by our friend Charles's place in Pennsylvania, and it was late around 3:00 a.m. and we met in a parking lot in a very small town and then a young guy driving by us called out to us. So we called back out to him, and he pulled up. We talked to him for a few minutes, and it turned out that he had been praying for a sign from God and that God set up our divine appointment and we lead him to pray the Sinner's Prayer and receive Christ and be filled with the Holy Spirit. It was amazing. We can never know where God will use us, but we can be sure that He is intentional in pursuing those who are seeking for Him.

We visited with our friend for a day or so and right, and he told us that his computer had just had the blue screen of death. Right before we were leaving, the Holy Spirit told me to give him my laptop. I was like, "That's a huge thing to do God and I need confirmation to know that it is You." So we start to leave and then I got it again and told Josh and God had spoken to Josh and gave me confirmation, and so we turned back around and I gave Charles my laptop in obedience to Christ.

We left Pennsylvania and headed back to Nashville, and when we had arrived, I was told that I could work a couple more days in the car and then I had to turn it back in. I turned it back in, and Josh and I rented a HyreCar and it was a Hybrid. We used it for a few days, and then it broke down while I was out driving. We got it back to the owner and switched out for another car, and then it broke down days later. Then we returned that car and rented a minivan from him and that minivan worked for one full day on a Saturday, and I was able to make $360, but at the end of the day, the van started over heating and was shaking and smoking, and my passengers were freaking out and thought it might explode. I told them they could get out if they want because traffic had me barely moving, and I couldn't do anything about it. I made it to the nearest O'Reilly's store and asked them to come out and take a look at the van. It turned out the van had no oil or coolant in it and so I bought both and put them in and headed back home and made it. After we turned the van in to the shop, we didn't want to rent anything else from the same guy, and for good reason.

Around this time, Josh's car was ready and so we rented another HyreCar, and we headed to Arkansas to pick his car up. We were able to pick it up, and because it was a Christian-owned shop, we were allowed to leave and make payments over time and they trusted us.

I had just heard a sermon on why to pray to God specifically for what we want in detail. Like with our earthly dad, we don't just ask for a car, we ask for what year, make, model, color, etc., we want from him, and with God, it is the same. We ask specifically because we believe that He is faithful to provide what we ask for. I decided to change my prayer, and so I asked God for a 2019 Alienware Flagship laptop in black. I prayed and I thanked Him in advance for the laptop I wanted.

I was hired by a woman making a movie in the Christian film industry to do distribution for her, and she paid me half up front according to what Holy Spirit spoke to her, and it was $2,500 and then Holy Spirit spoke to me and said, "Buy your laptop." I obeyed and was so mind blown as I picked it out and built it. One seed planted in obedience and God rewarded me with a top-of-the-line laptop worth double the value of the one I gave away! With a crucial tool to work on my other endeavors, I could begin working more on my graphic design, but I still needed transportation. So Josh and I shared his car for a while until I could figure out another option.

We began needing some car repairs related to alignment and tires, and we put a lot of money into the car. But we were getting behind and didn't know what we were going to do next, and so we prayed about it. The next day, God provided all Josh needed for his car repairs, and so we knocked it out in one fell swoop, the repair costs and his car payments! Wow. God provides our needs every time!

CHAPTER 20

COMPASSION

Willingness to suffer

My story was definitely not easy, but Luke 1:37 says, "With God all things are possible." One of the most important lessons I learned through all that I had been through is about compassion. *Compassion* in the Greek means "willingness to suffer." Matthew 9:36 (emphasis added) says, "But when He saw the multitudes, He was moved with *compassion* for them because they were harassed and scattered, like a sheep without a shepherd." The reason Jesus had compassion on the people is because He was willing to suffer with them in their humanity and was currently living the human experience and He *knew* their pain and suffering by firsthand experience. Every time Jesus saw people, it says that "He had compassion on them," and that led Him to feed them, give them water, heal the sick and diseased, and so much more.

I didn't understand why God allowed me to be molested. Why would a loving God allow me to endure such a terrible and traumatic experience? The answer is that the things that God allows are always geared toward our eternity. Also, if God had supernaturally intervened to stop him from doing that to me, it would have caused that man to live in constant fear the rest of his life. The same reason why Yahweh doesn't destroy Satan and the fallen angels, because then the holy angels would not be serving Him out of love and respect but out of fear. We sometimes question why God doesn't intervene against the actions of the sinful, but if the only option was to kill them or use supernatural means that they do not understand, then would he be a loving and holy God full of justice, mercy, and grace even for the sinner? Some things we may never understand, but in the eyes of God, His greatest concern is that we spend eternity with Him and will allow things in this earth that will cause the most people as possible to turn to Him and be saved from eternal damnation. In Matthew 28:17, Jesus says, "Hell was prepared for the devil and his angels." This is something that we must grasp and understand. Hell was never intended for humans. It's exactly the opposite. John 3:16–17 says, "For God so loved the world that He gave His only unique Son that whoever believes in Him will not perish but have eternal life. He did not send His Son into the world to condemn the world but that through Him, they would be saved."

The intentions of God all along were to provide the perfect solution to all problems and the perfect answer to all questions: Himself as a perfect sacrifice for each of us. The Word says *whoever* believes, and He has one desire for each of us: our heart to be loved by Him and to love Him. I spent years hating myself, performing to earn the love of God. Performing to prove my value and my worth to those around me but all along the greatest and highest price was paid for me by the sacrifice of the Son of God on the Cross. He says to each of us: "*You are loved.*" "*You are worthy.*" "*You are worth every drop of blood I shed, every breath I took, and every second of my life.*" "*You are irreplaceable to me.*" "*You are perfect to me just the way that you are.*" "*Come home into my loving arms sons and daughters.*" "*If you are weary and burdened by the cares and trials of this life come to me and I will give you rest and restore your soul.*"

You see if I had never been molested, how could I show compassion toward other people who had been molested without the experiential understanding of the suffering that they had endured? I had never been homeless, then I wouldn't be able to show compassion on the homeless from having been in their shoes. If I hadn't been addicted to drugs, then how could I love and understand others who are currently addicted to drugs from a kind and patient perspective without having felt the same feelings that they are currently feeling and the same desire to numb that pain in their hearts? If I hadn't been an alcoholic, then how could I understand what the root cause was that was causing that person to drink and drown their pain and sorrows in the first place? If I was never evicted, then how could I have compassion on someone who fell on hard times and was having to go through eviction because of circumstances outside of their control? If I was never in car accidents and had to learn how to trust God to protect me supernaturally, how could I teach others to trust God for their protection? If I was never behind on bills and rent due to the trials of this life, then how could I tell others to trust God to provide their every need? If I was never going without food, then how could understand what a starving person was feeling in order to move me in love to provide them with the food they need? If I had never suffered with depression and suicidal thoughts, then how could I tell someone currently going through that that things are going to get better? If I hadn't been arrested and taken to jail multiple times, then how could I show mercy and love to those who were misguided and made mistakes to get themselves into that situation? If I hadn't tried so many different drugs to get high such as marijuana, Xanax, Lortabs, cocaine, ecstasy, shrooms, Air Duster, bath salts, hydrocodone, skeletal muscle relaxers, and codeine-soaked blunts, then how could I testify that there is no high like the Most High and that those things only last as a moment of pleasure but in the end are just fleeting vanity that is leading to self-destruction? If I had never fallen in love and had my heart broken, how could I relate to those who go through the same thing? If I had never dealt with so many vehicle repairs, how could I be compassionate on those who are dealing with the same things? If I had never been used and manipulated because of my kindness and generosity, then how could I understand that feeling if someone else endured the same things? If I had never lost a close friend to suicide, then how could I lovingly be there for someone who also lost someone to suicide? If I had never had to quickly find a place to live, then how could I tell someone to trust God to open a door for them so that they wouldn't go homeless? If I had never cosigned for someone to get a vehicle and then had them flee, then how could I know the feeling of uncertainty that that brings into one's life? If I had never lived in my vehicle in the winter, then how could I show true love and compassion on someone in the same situation? If I had never been overworked at a job, then I would never have understood what that person is going through. If I had never been in a head-on collision and faced internal bleeding, then how could I understand the pain that people go through due to injury without having *felt* that pain? If I had never had to show mercy and forgive others in their sins and mistakes, then how could I tell other to show mercy and forgive those who sin against them? If I had never lived in a toxic and difficult environment with others, then how could I have compassion on those stuck in toxic environments? If I didn't acquire so much debt, then how could I encourage others to trust God to provide a way out without having experienced Him doing that for me firsthand? If I had not forgiven my molester and asked forgiveness of those who I had wronged and sinned against in my past, then how could I tell other people that they can also do that and be set free from years of addictions, anger problems, and all the other problems that caused them to endure? If I had not been hopeless and ready to end my life from jumping off a third-story balcony into the street on Madison Avenue in Memphis, TN, back in August of 2012 at the age of twenty-one years old and had I not gotten that phone call on my dad's phone that I borrowed that morning and had I not heard my sister pick up that phone and tell me all the miracles she experienced and how she had fallen off a horse at 30 mph and not be hurt, how her husband prayed to win the drawing at Guitar Center and he won a $500 grand prize to buy the microphones they needed for their worship music they recorded, had she not told me *"Leave no stone unturned in your life,"* then I wouldn't be here today and you would not be reading this incredible story that God has written using my life.

Compassion is a gift and don't allow your suffering to phase you and break you any longer because you are stronger than hell and stronger than the opposition you may be facing right now. Philippians 4:13 (emphasis added) says, "I can do *all things* through

Christ who strengthens me." Apostle Paul was beaten, thrown in prison, and endured terrible hardships but yet he also said in the two previous verses 11–12. Not that I speak because of lack, for I have learned in whatever state I am, to be content in it. I know how to be humbled, and I also know how to be in abundance. In everything and in all things, I have learned the secret both to be filled and to be hungry, both to abound and to be in need.

"I can do all things through Christ who strengthens me." Declare that over yourself right now, and if you are going through difficulties right now, then know you are not alone. If you have never met Jesus before and I don't mean the religious image of Jesus but the real and true Jesus, then I encourage you to join me in this journey with the most faithful and loving Father that we could ever imagine. Pray this prayer from the depths of your heart:

> Father God, I ask that you forgive me of my sins and that you would fill me with Your Holy Spirit right now. I believe that Jesus Christ is Lord and I ask You to be my Lord. I believe that He was crucified to be in relationship with me and that He was raised on the third day by the Father. Fill me with Your peace and bring restoration into every area of my life, provide all my needs, and open doors for me financially to be a blessing to others. Lord, use the circumstances that I have endured to refine me into a warrior for You and so that I will be an encouragement and an inspiration to those around me. In Jesus's name, Amen.

I want to also pray for you myself:

> Father God, touch the hearts of those who have prayed that prayer, bring healing to their hearts and minds, break chains and tear down

every wall and stronghold that Satan has built in their life, bring restoration and renewal to their souls and their families, help them to forgive those who have sinned against them so that they can be free, help them to trust you to provide their every need. I ask that You would go before them, Holy Spirit, and lead and guide them with their every decision moving forward in life and in this new life with You. Draw near to their hearts as they draw near to You, fill them with a hunger for Your Word, and I ask that You would place people in their lives to be an encouragement to them and to hold them accountable in their walk with You, that you would ignite a holy fire and zealous passion in their hearts and cover them with the anointing of Your presence, Your glory, and Your power. Baptize them in your Holy Spirit and *fire*, bring purification to their heart and life so that they can live a holy life and walk in victory and freedom. Break all witchcraft, hexes, vexes, curses, spells, incantations, and break every generation curse in their life and declare that it is broken *now*. In Jesus's name, Amen.

God renewed my body, reanimated my life, and restored every area of my life because I surrendered and had faith. Look at all the horrible things of my past life and just how powerful the love, grace, mercy, and faithfulness of God is!

Depression is gone from my life forever!! I am over seven years free from addiction! I feel joy down deep in my soul, and I feel peace that surpasses all understanding all the time! His presence has fulfilled and satisfied my longing desire when drugs, alcohol, pornography, sex, video games, cigarettes, or marijuana completely failed to take my pain away. Jesus took my pain away! I am free from anger problems and rage. I have no bitterness. I have the love of

God flowing through my veins! I am healed of all past shame, regret, pain, heartache, and perversion! I am ready to live with God as the unshakeable foundation of my life and peace and power of the Holy Spirit all around me. He's made me a new creation and He's the resting place we can run to and be made whole in His presence. No matter what you've done He will take you back. Turn to Him today while He can still be found. He loves you with an everlasting love and has only good things planned for you! You can trust Him and He will never leave you or forsake you! He accepts you in the midst of your struggles and wants to refresh you and give you rest. God bless you abundantly!

ABOUT THE AUTHOR

The author is from Memphis, Tennessee, and enjoys art, graphic design, song writing, and creativity of all kinds. He is now over seven years sober and has already led many people to freedom from their difficult pasts. He has many ministry projects he is working on and is the founder of All Consuming Fire Ministries and The World Hates Me apparel.

CPSIA information can be obtained
at www.ICGtesting.com
Printed in the USA
BVHW052054300921
617798BV00010B/124